Juggling For All

"POOR CHAP! HE LOST THREE BALLS IN LAST NIGHT'S SHOW"

Juggling For All

Colin Francome & Charlie Holland
Illustrated by Ali Bongo

First published in 1991 by Carla Publications

Carla Publications
Centre for Community Studies
Queensway
Enfield
Middlesex EN3 4SF
England

British Library Cataloguing in Publication Data
Francome, Colin
   Juggling for all.
   1. Jugglers and juggling.
   I. Title   II. Holland, Charlie
   793.8   GV1547

Printed and bound in Great Britain by
Redwood Books, Trowbridge, Wiltshire

To gravity, without which everyone
could juggle and this book wouldn't have
been written

Contents

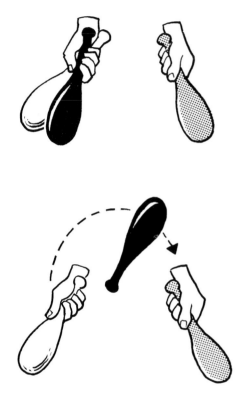

1 Introduction 9

2 Three ball juggling 13

3 Variations on three ball patterns 24

4 Juggling with clubs 35

5 Juggling with other objects 45

6 More advanced ball juggling 56

7 Juggling patterns for two people 62

8 Club passing 68

9 Getting an act together 75

10 Party tricks 82

11 Where do we go from here? 87

Distributors of juggling equipment 89

Acknowledgements 91

Index 93

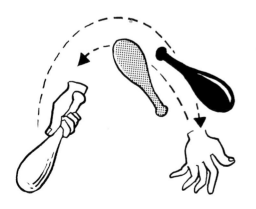

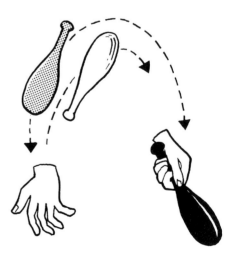

1 Introduction

Many people have admired the smooth movements of jugglers and wondered if they, too, could juggle. They may have been deterred by memories of embarrassing moments in sports where they have dropped the crucial catch and missed the opportunity to win a game. Such feelings should be overcome, however, for juggling is essentially non-competitive and allows individuals to develop their talents. It is also a great leveller. The greatest jugglers in the world still have occasions when their props are scattered all over the floor!

Who can juggle? – You can juggle

We believe that the simplest juggling tricks, and even some of the more advanced, can be mastered by anyone although some people will not find it easy to progress to the most difficult ones. However, the basics can be mastered by most. At parties we have even had six- and seven-year-old children juggling with us and participating in elementary routines. So we would recommend that you give juggling a try and in support we suggest a number of benefits.

The continuous motion of juggling is good exercise for the body. At first you can expect to do a great deal of bending down and picking up but, if it causes backache, try practising over a bed. Juggling is essentially light exercise which develops different parts of the body according to what movement is being performed. Some people have even taken to juggling while walking or jogging. Joggling, as it has been called, has been popular in the United States.

It is easy to take life too seriously and juggling is ideal for adding the fun element. It is a way of improving co-ordination without having to worry too much about how fast you progress in learning new movements or improving old tricks.

If you lack concentration then juggling will help improve it. For if you cease to concentrate your props will end up over the floor. Of course, some tricks need much more attention than others but a crucial factor in bettering your own performance is being able to concentrate for a period of time and apply extra attention for short periods when you are carrying out more difficult routines or movements.

Many people engage in various activities to try to relax from the trials of their working day or other problems. The qualities needed to improve juggling performance are regularity, smooth movements and a watchful eye and these all demand calmness. Juggling is not an explosive activity like long-jumping or throwing the javelin where the crucial part is one big effort. Rather it is the systematic practising of routines in a rhythmic manner and this in turn aids relaxation.

Whilst it can be a singular activity, we have found that people derive great pleasure from juggling together. They can help monitor each other's improvements and look out for any faults that might develop. Jugglers are generally sociable people who like to exchange ideas and help each other improve and there are growing numbers of juggling workshops and clubs. For those who wish to meet others there are details of some contacts at the end of this book.

Wherever you go in the world people appreciate juggling. So, if other forms of communication are difficult, it can be an ice breaker. We have found that juggling is an ideal way of meeting people when in new places.

The history of juggling

The art of juggling goes back at least as far as ancient Egypt and probably to even earlier times. A discussion of the early history of juggling was written by Max Koch in *The Juggler's Bulletin Annual* of 1952. He told of Socrates attending a banquet where a woman juggled with twelve hoops. However, Koch doubted whether she had them all going together because no modern juggler had beaten the record set by Eric Van Aro of ten hoops kept in the air.

The Latin word for a juggler is a *ventilator* and it seems that jugglers were popular in the early Roman Empire. On the monument to one such, Tagatus Ursus, it was claimed that he was the first juggler to use glass balls instead of the ordinary ones of the time and also that he had performed before large audiences in Rome. Other jugglers used lighted torches and Chrysostomus told in 347AD of a woman juggler in Antiochia who used pointed knives. In the thirteenth century manuscripts told of a juggler who worked on a rolling globe, while others in the Middle Ages balanced a heavy wheel on their shoulders when juggling with light objects or pebbles.

During the Renaissance jugglers, mime artists and jesters became increasingly popular and it seems that many were able to make a living from juggling by moving from town to town. Around 1700 travellers reported seeing Chinese jugglers balancing glass balls and spinning them on a stick. They also saw big basins being spun on the fingertips and this is still a feature of Chinese juggling today. In about 1770 a French performer, Mathieu Dupois, stood on the high wire and juggled with three apples which he caught on the points of forks at the end of his performance. One fork was held in each hand and the other in his mouth.

A famous juggler in the early part of the nineteenth century was Carl Rappo who was born in Innsbruck in 1800 and specialised in devil sticks (see page 53). In the late nineteenth century the development of the music hall as a source of entertainment meant that many jugglers could make a good living by appearing in these shows. Some stage jugglers learned a few tricks from the magicians to boost their act. A number of books published just after the turn of the century gave details of fake props which gave the appearance of being able to perform marvels. One of these was *Juggling Secrets* by Will Goldston, published in 1911. This book gave details of how to juggle and stressed the need for a great amount of practise. However, it also gave details of a number of fakes. One such was how to pretend to balance a tumbler on the edge of a card. Two cards were glued together and the back one was bent down the middle lengthways to make a hinge. The card is shown with the two cards placed together, then the hinge is opened to receive the tumbler which is placed on top.

Professor Ellis Stanyon's book, *New Juggling Tricks,* published in 1901, was very abrasive in style and stated in the preface:

It is my intention in this little book to expose some of the deceptions practised by the juggler of the present day and further to explain the construction of some of the apparatus he uses.

One of the tricks described was how to balance an egg on card. To do this two cards were stuck together with a piece of wire glued between them, slightly protruding at either end. This wire slipped into the groove placed in the end of a wooden egg painted white. The lower end of the card could then be placed onto a specially prepared wand with a groove so that no skill was needed. Professor Stanyon leaves the description of proper juggling to the later chapters.

Also written at the turn of the century was *The Art of Modern Juggling* by Anglo (T. Horton). He mentioned a number of tricks that are not often performed today. In one the juggler picks up three revolvers and fires them in turn before beginning to juggle. After they have been juggled four or five times they are fired each time they are caught. Anglo suggested that it would be virtually impossible to catch a normal revolver in such a way as to immediately pull the trigger. However, Hamley's sold special pistols with a steel rod attached from the trigger to the butt of the gun so that wherever it was caught on the handle it was only necessary to tighten the grip to fire it. He also mentioned other items, such as lamps, specially weighted swords, a juggling candle made from a metal tube and a wooden cigar with a little space for tobacco so that it could be smoked.

Anglo's book also contains a good description of what he called the 'Clumsy Juggler' and his instructions were:

Take three good size balls knock them together and drop them to show they are of solid wood then proceed to juggle with them from hand to hand for a few seconds throwing them higher and higher, and at last catch two of the balls and bow to your audience. To their horror they see the third ball desending on your head. Before they can give warning the catastrophe happens but the effect is merely that the last ball bounces softly off your head . . . When the rubber ball strikes the head knock the two other balls together sharply, giving the effect of a concussion with your cranium. As the rubber ball bounces again into the air catch it and continue to juggle as if nothing has happened.

This book was reviewed by Harry Houdini in *The Conjurer's Monthly* in March 1908 but Anglo unfortunately missed the review, for *The Juggler's Bulletin* of Sept 1904 contained the following article:

Messrs Hamley Bros of London England have sent us the following sad report of the sorrowful and untimely end of "Anglo", Australia's greatest juggler and Equilibrist. Anglo paid Messrs. Hamley a visit shortly before he sailed for his native land Australia. The terrible misfortunes which dogged his steps after his arrival there are best made known by means of extracts from his letter dated May 11 1904 at his majesty's gaol Adelaide.
"Dear Messrs Hamley: I thought that I would just drop you a line to tell you of my misfortune. Since I left London I have had varied luck. The first thing on landing at Adelaide I was greeted with the news of my wife's death which took place two days before. A few months after I married again and then my troubles commenced afresh. My second marriage was in every way a complete failure . . . She left me after we

had been married 3½ months and went home to her people . . . one Saturday night I met her in the street, I got wild and shot her dead. You may quite imagine my position then. I of course was put on trial and the jury brought a verdict against me. So tomorrow the 12 inst. I die. I do not think that I have any more to write about so will thank you in anticipation and wishing you all success and a long farewell."

Two of the greatest jugglers in the first half of this century were Rastelli and Cinguevalli. Enrico Rastelli, born in 1897, was both the son and grandson of jugglers. His father forebade him to become a juggler as they were poorly paid. However, Rastelli persevered and his act became so successful that in 1925, he was being paid £30 a day. He could juggle eight plates and was the first great juggler to appear in sports shirt and shorts. In one trick he balanced on one foot while rotating a hoop on his other ankle. He spun a ball on his right hand while juggling three sticks with his left hand and balancing a stick on his forehead. It is no wonder he practised for eight hours a day.

Paul Cinquevalli was a German who juggled commonplace objects. One routine with a teapot, a cup, a saucer and a lump of sugar finished with the cup on the saucer, the sugar in the cup and the tea poured from the pot. In a sequence called 'The Human Billiard Table' he made balls run up his arms and over his body until, by twisting and turning they landed in his pockets. He finished his act by catching a 48lb (22kg) cannonball on the back of his neck after it was dropped from a height of 40ft (12m).

The famous film comedian W. C. Fields started out in the performing world as 'The Eccentric Tramp Juggler'. He wore old torn clothing and looked unshaven. He is best known by jugglers for his skill with cigar boxes. However, one of his most difficult tricks was to balance a top hat, cigar and whisk broom on his foot. He would then kick them up so that the broom went into his back pocket, the hat on his head and the cigar into his mouth.

Juggling in the modern world

In recent years there has been an upsurge of interest in both watching and performing juggling. In the 1960s the San Francisco Mime Troupe used juggling and other circus skills to attract attention to their shows which expressed their political ideas. Much of the interest has been fostered by the enjoyment of seeing street entertainers who are able to reject a conventional lifestyle and travel round the world juggling. Gradually in towns, and at fairs and festivals, classes were set up and an international network developed.

The most successful of these new style jugglers are the Flying Karamazov Brothers, a group of five, who have been a major influence since their formation in the mid 1970s in California. They became the opening act for the archetypal 1960s band 'The Grateful Dead' and before long were appearing on Broadway. They dress as black clad, hairy Russians and are both talented and funny. Their shows revolve around juggling and include an element of danger, such as throwing chain saws at each other (not to be recommended) and music made by hitting drums with clubs.

Many jugglers relish the fact that they are involved in either a solo or team game which is essentially non-competitive as everyone is working together against gravity.

2 Three ball juggling

There are three basic juggling patterns from which hundreds of variations can be derived. This chapter describes how these patterns are performed and gives examples of tricks that can be developed from the basic moves. There are virtually limitless numbers of routines and new ones are still being discovered. The patterns we show here can be used as a basis from which you can build, using your own imagination and increasing ability. You will find some of these patterns easier to learn than others but it is difficult to predict which are likely to give most problems.

We describe the moves as a right-handed person would do them. If you are left-handed simply read right as left and left as right. As juggling is an ambidextrous skill the weaker hand will gradually become stronger and it sometimes helps to concentrate on your weaker hand. Counting the number of consecutive throws is a good way to measure improvement and it is a good idea to keep records of the number of catches without dropping with different tricks. Also, vary the speed and height of your juggling. A move done quickly and with little height looks different from the same one performed slowly and with high tosses.

WHAT TO JUGGLE WITH

When learning, it is best if the objects used are relatively soft so that they do not hurt you if you drop them on yourself, are the right size for handling and are not so bouncy that they run away when you drop them. It may also help to use different colours so that you can see the movement of each ball. Beanbags are ideal. They are usually made slightly smaller than a tennis ball and are filled with pearl barley or rice. Some people like tennis balls, and they are good for heading movements, but they are a little light and will roll away. It is possible to avoid these effects by making an incision and filling them with pearl barley before glueing the cut. Rubber dog balls are a good size and weight and are durable, but they are a little hard and bouncy.

As you progress you may consider buying larger more visible balls (normally called stage balls) and special balls for bounce tricks. Canadian lacrosse balls are used by many jugglers and the best are silicon balls which are specially made for jugglers but are expensive. Of course, many jugglers began their career with the family fruit which they quickly made into a sticky mess while others have started with three small stones or pebbles from the garden.

The three basic patterns

These are called the cascade, in which the balls seem to cross in mid air, the shower, where the balls follow each other round in a circle, and columns, where the balls rise and fall parallel to each other.

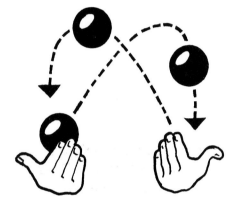

The cascade

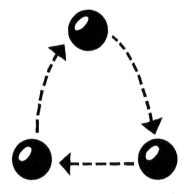

The shower

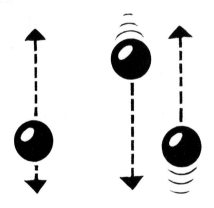

Columns

THE CASCADE

The cascade is the easiest pattern to learn and also the most rhythmic. It is the pattern jugglers usually return to between tricks.

Step one: the throwing action

A most important rule in juggling is that if the throw is right the catch will look after itself. It is important to make all throws as accurate as possible. Take one ball and practise tossing it in an easy arc from one hand to the other. The ball should be thrown from about waist height to a point level with the top of your head. The hands should make an inward scooping action for the throw. The balls from either hand will have a different trajectory and this will help avoid the balls meeting or kissing in the air.

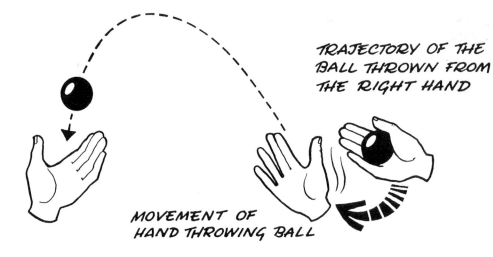

TRAJECTORY OF THE BALL THROWN FROM THE RIGHT HAND

MOVEMENT OF HAND THROWING BALL

Cascade step one: the throwing action

Step two: two balls

Hold one ball in each hand, throw the right hand ball in an arc towards your left hand and, as it peaks, throw the second ball in an arc underneath it towards the right hand. Catch the first ball in your left hand and the second in your right.

Make sure each ball is thrown to the same height. Many people instinctively pass, rather than throw, the second ball from their left hand to their right, or else throw both up together instead of one at a time. If you have difficulty getting the throws right, practise throwing without attempting to catch the balls at all. Practise starting with alternate hands and place most emphasis on your weaker hand. This will help you when you try three balls.

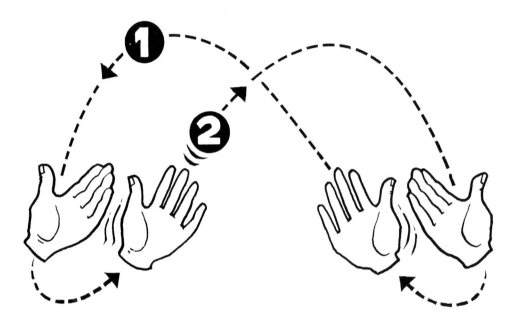

Cascade step two: two balls

Step three: three balls

Hold two balls in your right hand and one in your left. Toss the first ball in your right hand towards your left one and, as it peaks, throw the ball in the left hand towards the right and catch the first ball in your left. As the second ball peaks, throw the final ball from your right hand, before catching the second ball in your right hand. Keep on repeating this sequence and you are juggling.

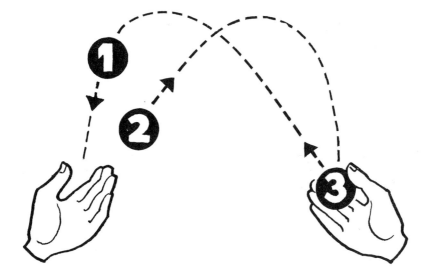

The cascade complete

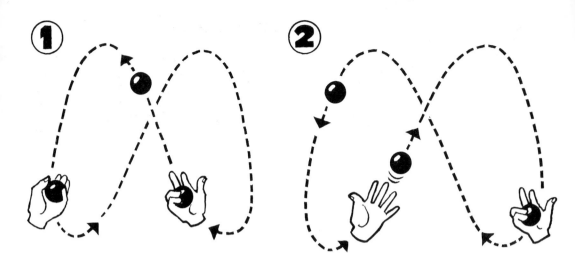

The cascade with three balls

Very few people manage to juggle at the first attempt and if you are one of the many whose brain and hands seem unable to work together the following tips may help:

1 Remember that for most of the time only one ball is in the air, with two being there only for the brief time while one ball is entering your hand and the other is leaving it (as shown in the diagram).

2 Go back to step two and try to visualise the same move with three balls.

3 Take three balls and practise the throwing action, without any attempt to catch the balls, so that you can see the points they should reach and learn the sequence of the throws.

4 If you find that you are throwing the balls forward and having to move to catch them, try making more of a scooping action and, standing in front of a wall, concentrate on making the balls peak at a fixed distance from the wall.

5 A weaker hand can be strengthened by extra practise. If you are right-handed then it is a good idea to throw a ball against a wall at a relatively short distance, using only your left hand. To begin with you can face the wall but, after a while, if you stand sidewards on to it, you can simulate the pattern that would be used in juggling.

6 If you have difficulties in obtaining a rhythm and find problems in throwing the ball to the required height all the time, you need to try and relax, and get into a regular pattern. Sometimes patience is needed to gradually develop the necessary skills.

7 It is also possible to resolve problems with catching. Beginners usually find that the balls smack into their hands, instead of dropping into them gently as the hand is moved up to catch the ball and drawn down with it. Some people find it is useful to begin each session with a warm up where they toss single balls so that they can get their eye in before they begin juggling.

8 If you find that the balls are kissing in the air frequently it may be because you have not sorted out the flight paths correctly. If this is the case it is a good idea to practise with one and then two balls tossing them from hand to hand in the correct formation. This kind of practise can also help in developing rhythm of movement.

COLUMNS

With columns juggling the balls go up and down, parallel with one another, instead of crossing each other's flight path. The hands move towards the descending ball instead of the ball being thrown to the hand.

Before juggling three balls in columns you need to be able to juggle two balls in one hand. There are three patterns to practise:

a The inward scoop

Hold both balls in your right hand. Throw one up and a little to the right. Throw the second one up immediately afterwards and move your hand to the right to catch the first one. Then scoop inwards and throw it up again, returning your hand to the right place to catch the second ball. Continue in this manner.

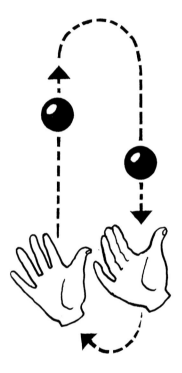

The inward scoop

b The outward scoop

This is the same as the inward scoop, except that you throw the balls so that they go up and slightly to the left and your hand scoops the other way to catch them.

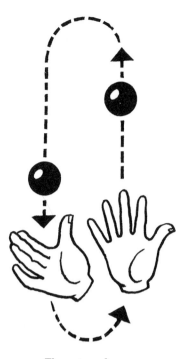

The outward scoop

c The column

Here the balls are thrown up and down parallel to each other while the hand moves in a horizontal plane to catch and throw them.

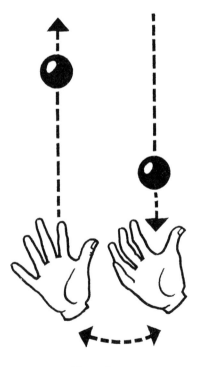

The column

Practise these moves until you can do them competently with either hand. Now take two balls in your right hand and one in the left. Throw the first ball from your right hand straight up and, as it peaks, throw the other two balls up on a parallel path either side of it. Catch the first one in your right hand and throw it straight back up again. The right hand is doing the column move while the left hand throws one ball in time with the second ball to leave the right hand.

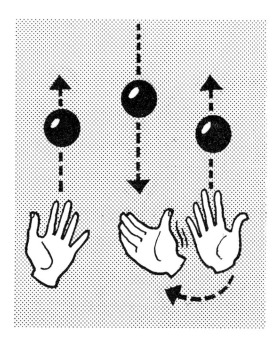

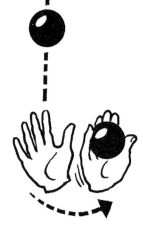

Basic column moves

When you have mastered this, try catching the middle ball with the left hand instead of the right. Then, alternate control of the middle ball between the left and right hands. As you master this you can start to move the middle ball around, throwing it up to the right, or the left, of the other two balls. Try also throwing one up the middle and the other two across it. Sometimes they hit and bounce back into the hands from which they were thrown.

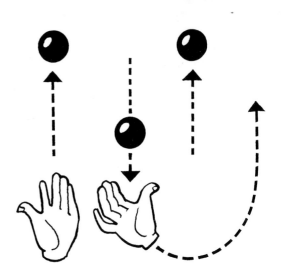

On catching the ball, bring the hand to the right of the ball in the air and toss it back up again

Balls kissing in the air and bouncing back

THE SHOWER

The motion of the balls with this trick is totally different from that of the cascade. In the shower the balls go round in a circle and, unlike the cascade, there are two balls rather than one in the air for most of the time. To begin with hold two balls in the right hand and one in the left. The two balls in the right hand are tossed in the air in rapid succession, making an arc about 2ft (65cm) high, aiming to come down to the left hand. Just as the second ball is leaving the right hand the one in the left hand should be moving to the right hand. It is caught by the right and im-mediately tossed up in the circular motion. In the shower the eyes are concentrated at the top of the arc and this enables you to judge where the ball approaching the left hand is going to land. However, the pass from the left to the right hand is carried out without any vision whatsoever and, to minimise the possibility of mistakes, the hands need to be brought together for the pass.

This movement is more complicated than the cascade and is more difficult for most people. However, we have known beginners who found the shower easier to do as the movement came more naturally to them.

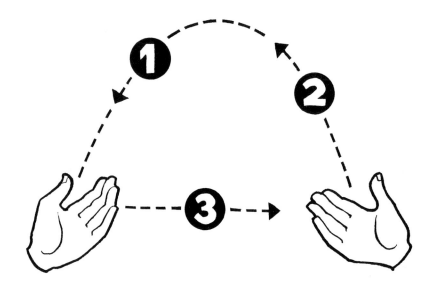

The shower

3 Variations on three ball patterns

Juggling with three balls gives the most opportunity for variation and comedy. It obviously pays to begin with the easiest movements but, once you have mastered a few tricks, it is a relatively simple matter to combine them together into a routine. The easiest way to start is to introduce variations of height. By tossing one of the balls high in the air the juggler has time to look around or engage the audience before continuing with the routine. The high toss can also be used to help move around and once this simple manoeuvring has been accomplished, a number of other tricks may be tried.

Heading the ball while juggling

Tossing the ball high and then catching it is important practice for heading the ball. Discovering the time this takes enables you to slot in the heading of the ball without disturbing your overall juggling rhythm. A second part of the practice is to take one ball and toss it from your right hand onto your forehead and then into your left hand, aiming to head the ball as smoothly as possible and to build up a sequence. Expert soccer players will clearly find this process easier than others. One important point to remember is to watch the ball closely and not to blink at the vital moment, so losing sight of it as it travels to the other hand.

Once the variations of height and bounce have been learned separately they can be combined and heading the ball can be included in your repertoire. When practising it is also a good idea to count how many times you can head the ball without any drops.

When you are proficient at single heading it may be time to consider continuous heading. This entails rapidly moving the head from side to side as each ball is thrown up in turn and headed which can be very amusing for onlookers, as well as being enjoyable for you.

Three ball flash

In this pattern all three balls are in the air at the same time, leaving the hands empty for a fraction of a second. Juggle in the cascade pattern and throw the balls faster and higher than usual – right, left, right – and try to clap your hands before catching them – left, right, left. Then continue the cascade. Try also performing the flash by beginning with the left hand. The flash is a useful way of building up to five ball juggling and is also very impressive if a pirouette is done while the balls appear to hang suspended in mid air.

Under the leg

One of the easiest tricks to learn is throwing a ball under a leg while juggling. You need to raise your right leg and throw the ball in the right hand underneath it and up to the usual peak above the left hand. It will take a few times to get the rhythm of raising the leg and the timing of passing the ball underneath it.

Reverse cascade

This is a basic cascade pattern except that the hands make an outward scooping motion and throw the ball over, rather than under, the incoming one.

Because the balls are being thrown over the incoming ones they tend to go higher and wider than normal. Gradually you can refine the reverse cascade until it takes up no more air space than the ordinary one. Avoid throwing the ball so far over the top that the hand catching it has to move out from the body. The balls should be caught just in front of the trunk and the hands scoop outwards to throw the balls over the incoming one.

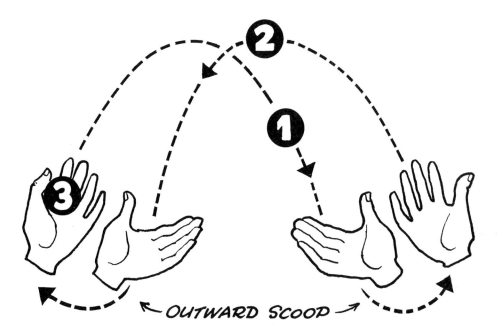

Reverse cascade

Moving while juggling

Once you have managed to juggle success-fully standing still you can become a little more adventurous and start to move around. If you want to give a show it is more interest-ing for an audience to see some mobility. The secret is simply to throw the ball in the direc-tion you are going and move towards it to catch it. One quite amusing movement is to toss the ball directly over your head with plenty of height. There will then be time to complete the necessary half turn to catch the ball and repeat the process if desired.

You can experiment with a number of ac-tivities while trying to keep the balls in the air. These include going down on each knee alternately, going down on both knees, sitting down and even lying down flat on the ground. To lie down while juggling you first need to go down on both knees. Then one is gradu-ally slid forward and the other tucked up under the body so that the lower parts of the legs are at right angles to each other. From this position it is a relatively simple matter to sit down. Both the legs can then be placed to-gether and you can lie down by controlling the stomach muscles. The head will need to be slightly raised to see the balls.

To get up from this position sit up and bring up one of your legs. Right-handed people will probably find it easier to bring up the left leg so that the foot is placed under the right knee. Then, in order to stand up, a gentle rocking motion is needed to give a little momentum. As a comedy item in a show it is a good idea to make a few pretences of being unable to get up before finally managing to do it.

Juggling behind the back

This is a more spectacular trick in that the ball moves out of sight for a period of time. The main exercise to practise for this is to toss one ball over the shoulder and catch it in the opposite hand, and then alternate. So, starting with the right hand, swing your arm behind your back, toss the ball over the left shoulder and catch it in the left hand. The first few times you try this you must expect the ball to hit the shoulder, the wall or the ceiling. Prac-tise until you can catch the ball in your left hand, throw it behind your back to clear the right shoulder and into the right hand to com-plete the sequence. If you plan to toss the ball from your right hand over the left shoulder throw the ball from your left hand higher than usual. This will present the extra time that is necessary for you to toss the ball in your right hand over the shoulder and return to catch the ball from the left hand. It is best to prac-tise one shoulder at a time and improvement can be monitored by counting how many moves can be made correctly in succession. It is also possible to keep one hand behind your back and juggle the normal cascade pattern, as shown in the diagram.

Juggling behind the back

Bouncing a ball off various parts of the body

Many people can manage the trick of holding a ball in their hand, tossing it up and bouncing it off the inside of their elbow. The secret of getting a good bounce is to slightly bend the arm and then straighten it at the moment of impact. This movement can be successfully incorporated into a juggling routine by giving the ball a little extra height to leave the time to bend the elbow ready to bounce the ball. It is also possible to bounce from one arm to the other. Another bounce is that off the knee or upper thigh. This is fairly simple although regularly bouncing from one thigh to the other is quite difficult to master.

Other bounces, such as from the shoulder or onto the foot, are more difficult and can only be mastered after a great deal of practise.

Catching the ball in the elbow or on the neck

To catch the ball in the elbow you will need to give the balls a little extra height. If you plan to catch the ball in the right elbow, throw the ball from your left hand a little higher. Then raise the right elbow to meet the ball and bring it down at a slightly slower pace than the ball is travelling. The ball then gently rests in the crick of the elbow and can be tossed up again to resume juggling.

Catching the ball in the neck is more difficult and is best practised with only one ball. One crucial feature of this trick is to hold the ball directly in front of the body and toss it at right angles towards the body, just as if you were going to head the ball. When the ball is about 6in (15cm) from your head raise your shoulders and stretch your neck up to make a pocket to catch the ball. As you do this gradually lower your trunk and bend your knees so that the ball nestles on the back of your neck. Both your arms will be positioned in an inverted 'V'. To flick the ball up to resume juggling nod your head forward and then bring it sharply back. The ball will roll slightly forward as you bring your head down and will then be propelled into the air. To do this while juggling it is important to have the balls moving smoothly and for the ball not to be thrown too high. (See the picture on page 77.)

The dummy

Juggle two balls in the right hand in the columns pattern. Instead of throwing and catching the ball in your left hand in synchronisation with one of the balls in your right hand, move the left hand up and down just holding the ball. It should move at the same time and to the same height as it is normally thrown. If done well it takes several moments for the onlooker to notice the cheat action. The ball should be held so that it is clearly visible, face on, to the onlooker.

The yo-yo

This is the same move as the dummy except that the cheat ball is held about 6in (15cm) above the left of the two balls juggled in the right hand. It is moved up and down with this left hand ball and looks as though the lower ball is joined to it by a string.

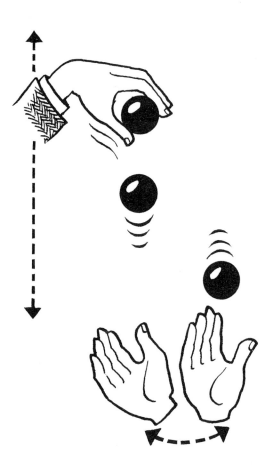

The yo-yo

The yo-yo with no strings

Gradually you will gain confidence in moving the left hand in conjunction with the right-hand juggle and can gauge the height of the right hand throws accurately. You should be able to spot a gap in the right hand juggle where one ball is peaking and the other is still in the hand. This presents an opportunity to move the left hand, holding the cheat ball, through the middle without interrupting the juggling pattern. Having got the left hand across wait until you can spot the gap again and bring the ball back. Alternatively, try circling the cheat ball around the right hand ball in the juggle. Finally try moving the cheat ball across and back in a single gap.

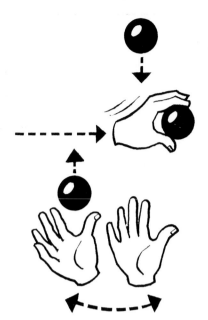

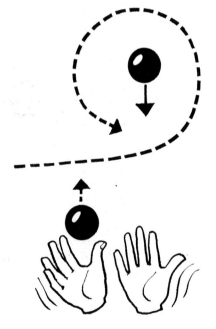

The yo-yo with no strings

The chop

Cascade three balls and with your right hand catch one of the balls higher in the air than usual. Then, bring it down across the body in a chopping action as shown in the diagram before throwing it out. To prevent the second ball being hit by the chop as it leaves the left hand, scoop this hand further to the right. This allows the ball to be thrown underneath the hand making the chop. The higher you throw the second ball the more exaggerated and visually effective the chop can become.

Practise this move until you can do the chop on every throw with your right hand. Also, learn the chop with your left hand (the actions are the same but done as a mirror image of the right hand chop). Ultimately you will find you can chop continuously with your right, then left, then right hand. This is a move that requires fast reflexes and accurate throws so it will take time to perfect, but its visual appeal makes the effort worthwhile.

ARROW INDICATES 'CHOP' MOVEMENT OF RIGHT HAND

THE LEFT HAND IS ABOUT TO MOVE BACK TO CATCH BALL № 1

The chop

The overhead cascade

Stand with your hands slightly above your head, palms raised as though supporting a low ceiling that is about to collapse. Take one ball and hold it in the finger of one hand in the above position. Flick it up so that it can be caught by the other hand with minimal movement and practise flicking it to and fro between the two hands. If you find yourself throwing the ball forwards you probably need to lean back a bit more. When you are competent at doing this with one ball try with three. As your ability grows you can practise kneeling and then lying down flat from a standing start while maintaining the overhead cascade.

The train roll

The juggler kneels down and cascades the balls in very small arcs. Then, at some point, the ball leaving the right hand is rolled along the ground towards the left and the subsequent balls are also rolled in the same fashion so the balls are moving in a circular motion.

The three balls in one hand start

In this trick, which starts off a juggle, all three balls are thrown up at once and snatched from the air. To do this you hold three balls on the palm and fingers of your hand. One ball should be forward of the other two and held only by the fingers. The other two are side-by-side, secured by the thumb and little finger. When you throw the balls up the forward ball will go higher than the others and is, therefore, the last ball to be caught. The other two balls go up parallel with each other and your right hand rises with them, snatches the right hand ball down and scoops it out as the first throw in the cascade. The left hand catches the left hand ball and throws it out. The third ball is caught as normal by the right hand and the cascade is completed.

When you have mastered this, try also starting with your hand under a leg, throwing the three balls up and bringing your hand back so you start to juggle in a normal stance. You can also try putting your arm behind your back and doing the one hand start, tossing the balls over your shoulder. One ball will travel much higher than the other two and can be caught last or, alternatively, you can head it before moving into the cascade.

Animal patterns

THE GORILLA

Juggle in the cascade pattern, and in the time you hold a ball in your hand before throwing it out, swing your arm in and beat your chest once before throwing the ball out from the usual position. Practise this with both right and left hands until you can do it fluently, alternating every right and left beat. Add a suitable gorilla-like pose and expression or shout Ta-a-arza-a-an.

THE PENGUIN

This move, based on the cascade, is hard to master. Hold your left arm stiffly down by your side with your wrist and elbow twisted clockwise and your palm facing up, your fingers splayed away from your body. Throw a ball from your right hand and try to catch it with minimal movement from your left arm. Next turn your wrist anti-clockwise and flick the ball up in front of you, using only your wrist and fingers, to the right hand still keeping the left hand by your side. Now do the opposite – holding your right hand by your side. Juggle three balls and, while the incoming ball is peaking, twist your left arm round as above, catch the ball and flick it back into the juggle. Build this skill up until you can do it with either arm and with every throw.

The final step is to stand with your legs together, feet splayed out and both arms rigid by your sides flicking the balls from side to side in a constant stiff-arm cascade. By slightly stretching your imagination you can picture yourself as a penguin shaking water off your feathers after a swim. To complete the picture try waddling forwards at the same time.

The penguin

THE GIRAFFE

This is a shower pattern performed with the left hand held high, 3 to 4in (7-10cm) in front of you. The right hand balls need to be thrown extremely accurately so that they fall into the left hand from just above it. The left hand drops the balls straight down to the right hand just as the incoming ball peaks. Throughout this pattern the left arm should not move at all, except for very slight corrections.

The giraffe

4 Juggling with clubs

Once you have mastered the cascade with three balls you can think about moving on to clubs. There are several kinds of clubs on the market but to start with you may like to make your own. This can be done fairly simply and is described later in this chapter.

To start with clubs toss one in the air and try to catch it again after just one spin. Hold the club in your hand pointing upwards at about a 45° angle. Lower your hand slightly and smoothly bring it up, letting go of the club when your arm is parallel to the ground. Most of the movement should come from the arm with very little wrist action. You should try and make the club go vertically up so that you do not have to move your feet to catch it nor duck out of the way as it approaches your head. The club is caught naturally between the thumb and fingers and, as you receive it, bring your hand down so that it does not jar and you are in a position to continue. To get the right spin is a matter of practice and adjusting the arm and wrist movements, but it should only take a matter of minutes.

You can then practice passing the club with one spin between the hands. If you start with the club in the right hand you throw it in front and across your body at about an angle of 45°, catch it by bringing your left hand down and throw it back, trying to make the height, spin and speed of the club consistent between the hands. This consistency will become increasingly important as you increase the number of clubs you juggle at one time.

Having learnt the club catch there are two ways of proceeding which complement each other. The first is to use one club and two balls in the cascade pattern. The advantage of this is that, as you have already mastered the cascade, it is relatively easy to fit in the club. Also if the throw does go awry you are more able to gain control than if you were juggling straight away with three clubs.

After mastering the one club it is a good idea to practise with two. Hold one club in each hand and throw the club from right hand towards the left. Immediately this club has left your hand bring the left hand down and throw the club underneath the approaching club and into the right hand. Now wait a beat where, if you had three clubs, the other club would have been thrown. This movement is sometimes called vamping and is very good preparation for the insertion of the third club.

Another useful exercise with two clubs is to hold them both in your right hand and practise throwing one of them with one spin to the left hand. The club to be thrown first should be held between the tip of the thumb and the tips of the fingers above the second club as shown in 'A' in the diagram. Some people may benefit from spending some time juggling with two clubs and one ball but others who are anxious to move on may prefer to go straight to juggling three clubs.

With the above preparation juggling three clubs should follow naturally. In fact many people find they are less likely to drop clubs because their weight and spin allow for a firmer grip than with balls. The pattern of the clubs follows that of the balls in terms of there being two adjacent 'hills' so that, at least in theory, the clubs will not collide. In practice, of course, you may expect to find the clubs crashing into each other on occasions and also have problems with the degree of spin and the heights of the throws. However, just as with balls, your improvement can be monitored by counting the number of throws between drops.

It is also important to learn how to stop the three club cascade without dropping the clubs on the floor. You can then do a number of catches and stop. The easiest method for this is to catch the club in the air in your right hand on top of the one that is already there. As you prepare for the catch you tuck the first club up under the base of your thumb and

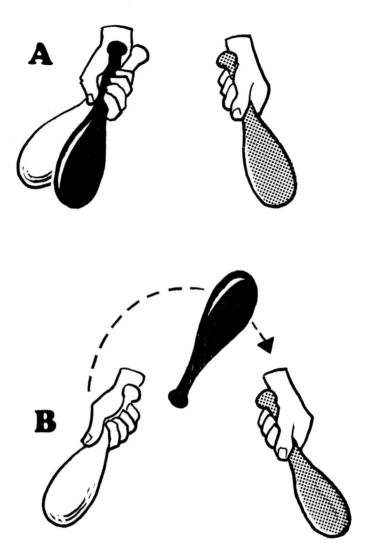

stretch out your fingers. The two clubs will smack together as you catch them and you will be in the position to start again.

Once you have been able to get the cascade going reasonably proficiently it is time to experiment with double and, later, triple spins. To do a double spin bring your hand down a little lower than for a single spin and toss the club up with slightly greater arm movement and so greater height. However, the main difference between the double and single spins comes from extra twist from the wrist. It is best to try this with just the single club until you are fairly proficient and are catching the right end of the club. Once you can judge the double spin with a degree of

confidence you can introduce it into the cascade, gradually increasing its frequency until eventually you should be able to do a full cascade of doubles.

For the triple spin just increase the arm and wrist movements to give the height needed for the extra turn. One of the advantages with specially made juggling clubs that makes this catch easier is that when they are spinning the handles stick out further than the heads and so you are unlikely to catch the head by mistake. It is possible to do a whole shower of triple spins but this takes a great deal of space and may be a problem in many rooms.

One great advantage of this trick is that it

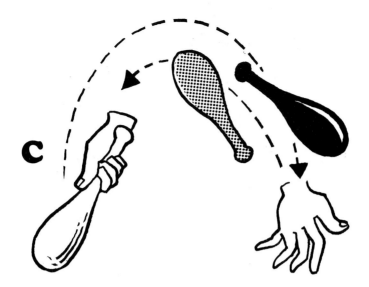

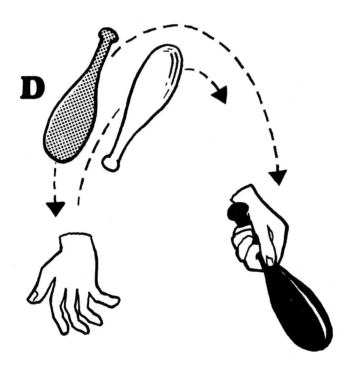

Juggling three clubs

enables you to do an alternative finish. The extra time available while the spinning club is in the air allows you to transfer your left hand club to the right hand. With both the stationary clubs together you have a hand free to catch the third club and finish. This is a spectacular way of stopping and is more suitable for ending a display than simply catching two clubs in the right hand. You could also be going down on to one knee before catching the triple and striking a dramatic pose.

It is relatively easy to make a set of juggling clubs. Use broom handles cut into 18in (45cm) lengths and lightweight plastic lemonade bottles or, alternatively, the Americans recommend bleach bottles. For a slightly narrower grip the handles from discarded sponge mops might be more suitable than the broom handles. Stick the handle to the bottom of the container and screw it in place. At the Cornwall folk festival in 1985 the children's workshop made clubs with sawdust placed in the head to give a little extra weight but still making them very soft in case they inadvertently hit someone. The hole at the neck of the bottle can be tacked and then filled with masking tape to make sure it is secure. For added comfort the handle can be covered with sponge pipe lagging or other cloth material.

For a more sophisticated looking set of clubs use a set of plastic bowling pins from your local toy store; Mothercare make a useful set. There are, of course, various kinds of professionally made clubs on the market and details of where to obtain them are given on page 89.

Tricks with three clubs

UNDER THE LEG
a) By raising the leg
This is a fairly simple trick. While you are in the cascade pattern simply bring your right hand slightly lower than normal and at the same time lift your right leg into the air. You then should have the space to throw the club underneath and continue juggling. Learn this with your other hand and leg and it is possible to walk around a room, albeit slowly, tossing the clubs under alternate legs.

It is also possible to throw the club from the right hand under the left leg. The position of the feet is the same as above but the body sways to the right this time. Quite a spectacular routine is to throw the clubs from each hand alternatively under one leg.

b) By keeping both legs on the floor
To throw the club forwards under the left leg with both feet on the ground first take half a step forward with your left foot. It should be at right angles to your body and about 12-14in (30-35cm) in front of the right. The right foot is turned slightly outwards and both legs are bent. Your body bends backwards to the left. It is a rather awkward position for those who tend to suffer from cramp but the rest of the movement is similar to throwing behind the back. As you throw the club under your leg from your left hand you need to give extra height to the club leaving your right. The club from the right hand should not be thrown as far across the body as usual. Once the single throws have been mastered you can attempt continuous throws.

BEHIND THE BACK

To accomplish this you need to begin by tossing a single club from your right hand behind your back and over the shoulder into the left hand. It helps if you lean slightly over to your right as you prepare to make the throw. In order for the club to come nicely to hand the wrist movement must be slowed. In this way it will reduce the spin and bring the club to the correct position. For symmetry it is useful to then try and go back the other way, from the left hand over the right shoulder. Once you are proficient at this movement it is time to work it in to your cascade. While preparing to throw the club over your left shoulder with your right hand you should throw the club from your left one with extra height to give the added time needed. As you lean to the right throw the club over your left shoulder, catch it and continue with your cascade.

There are a number of ways this movement can be worked into a routine. The first is to do the throw continuously, but it is more effective to throw over each shoulder alternately. The body is then moving from left to right to make the throws and so there is greater variety. It is possible to throw the clubs alternately over the shoulders while going round in a circle. To move round to the left, throw the clubs over the right shoulder with extra spin and slightly more towards the centre of the body, then turn the feet to the left. The club from the right hand is thrown slightly more to the left than usual.

COLUMNS

For this pattern you need to practise juggling with two clubs in one hand. There are two ways of doing this. One is to throw them in a circular motion, but far easier and more relevant for this trick, is to send the clubs up and down in columns with one spin between each catch. When you have accomplished this on a regular basis it is fairly easy to throw a single club from the other hand in time. This pattern looks amusing when one of the clubs is thrown in the air on its own to the left hand side and then the body and feet move over to catch two other clubs thrown over to the right.

PLACING A CLUB UNDER THE ARM OR BETWEEN THE LEGS

At some point during the routine throw one club a little higher than usual to give you a chance to place the club already in your hand under your arm and wedge it close to the body. You can catch the club in the air, stop juggling and suggest that you do not know where the third club has gone. Similarly, the trick can be done with a club placed between the legs. Charlie regularly does this with fire clubs, placing the lighted end behind him, and so far he has not caught his trousers alight.

REVERSE CASCADE

This is similar to that described for three balls. In a normal cascade you catch the clubs and move the hands inwards for the next throw. So, at some point during the routine, you need to move your hands outwards and throw the club over the top of the incoming club. A reverse cascade needs about twice the height of a normal cascade and so the clubs are thrown with very little wrist movement and greater than usual arm movement. When you do the reverse cascade you will probably find that you drop the clubs a great deal at first as they come down at an unusual angle.

OVER THE HEAD

While you are in the cascade you can suddenly toss a club backwards over your head with three spins, quickly turn round to catch the club and then continue juggling. After two throws of the clubs the process is repeated so that you are continuously moving round. If your room does not allow sufficient height you can slightly alter the movement and throw the club with only two spins. This will mean that you have less time and so will probably need to throw the club slightly over your shoulder to catch the club before you have turned round 180°. You can complete the turn with the extra throw of the clubs.

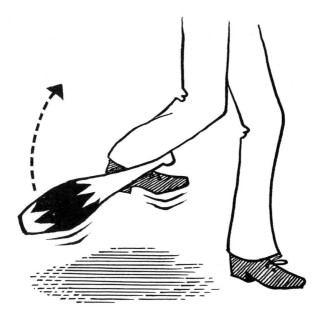

Club kick-up

OUTSIDE FOOT KICK-UP

This trick can be a start but can also take place during a routine. We have found that kick-ups are very difficult to do with leather shoes so it is best to wear canvas ones or go barefoot. To kick up from your right foot place the neck of the club across the foot so that the head of the club points out to the right. Stretch your toes up to hold the club in place. Step forward with your left foot and your right shin will then be angled forward. Then raise your right leg sharply under you, raising your knee and bringing your heel up under your behind. The club handle gets caught in the angle and you can catch it after a single spin.

The kick-up is useful in a routine as an escape from an accidental drop. In fact it works so well, many jugglers drop on purpose so they can incorporate it.

A number of possible problems can arise with this trick. First, if the floor is slippery the club can slide out of position. For this reason some professional jugglers place a small mat on the floor to create the necessary friction. Secondly, your shoes may be too slippery. Also, it can slow a routine up. But, on the other hand, it is spectacular and brings variety to any juggling routine. It is especially suitable for a comedy routine where the juggler is going to fail on the first two attempts.

FLATS

This is where a club does not spin at all when it is thrown. Instead of the normal action, where the head is made to rise, the handle is pushed upwards somewhat so that the club goes across without spinning.

THE BALANCE

Here you hold one club horizontally in your left hand and balance another vertically on top of it so that the knob of the upright one is about half way along the body of the horizontal one. Remember that it is easiest to control the balance if you concentrate on watching the top of the object being balanced. When you can hold this balance easily you can try to achieve it during a juggle. Do the cascade as normal and throw a double from the right hand straight up. Then quickly place the next club in the right hand on to the left hand club before catching the double spin club in the right hand again.

As an additional trick, try flicking over the club being balanced so that it lands on its head, on the lower club.

The club balance

THE HELICOPTER

This is a real crowd-pleaser, especially when done with torches. The effect is of the main rotor blade rotating between the smaller vertical blades at the end of the helicopter. To accomplish this trick, practise juggling two clubs in the left hand on double spins in an outward circle pattern as described earlier with balls. Practise separately swinging a club over your head in a horizontal plane, holding it by the knob. When you are confident with both these moves you can attempt to do them together. You need to time the sweep of the right hand club so that it passes between the other two just as one is peaking and the other is in the hand.

THIS CLUB SWEPT HORIZONTALLY AROUND ABOVE THE HEAD

TWO CLUBS JUGGLED VERTICALLY, PARALLEL TO EACH OTHER

The helicopter

JUGGLING ONTO A TOM-TOM DRUM

This is something Colin has done in his act for many years. It is not necessary to use a drum – it could be a tambourine or, even, for practice purposes a table or chair will do. The juggling is the usual cascade but when you are about to strike the drum you hold the club a little more firmly. Give a quick tap and keep control ready for the throw. By varying the intervals between the strikes you can create a rhythm and it is possible to get an audience to sing in time to the drumming.

FANCY STARTS

Two club beginning

There are at least three ways to start juggling by throwing the first two clubs up together. Possibly the easiest is to hold two clubs in your right hand and one in your left. Then toss a club from each hand into the air with a single spin. When these two are just in the air toss the third one to the right of them with a single spin. The first clubs are caught in the hands that threw them and from there you can move easily into a cascade. A second method is slightly more spectacular in that the third club is thrown with a double spin. The main problem with this is that you do not have the time to throw the double with the usual arm movement and so you have to use a great deal of wrist movement for control.

In the third method the two clubs in the right hand are tossed up together. They go into the air with enough height for one spin. Immediately afterwards the club in your left hand is thrown with a double spin to the side of the first two clubs. Catch one of the first two in each hand, then catch the third one coming down and start juggling. You may have some problems with the first two clubs colliding with each other so it is worthwhile spending some time just throwing the two clubs up and catching them in either hand. There may also be a tendency for the third club to be thrown forward and this can be corrected by a little extra wrist movement.

Three club beginnings

Grip the handles of the three clubs between your two hands so that they are sticking out horizontally before you. There should be two parallel together with the third resting on top.

The third club needs to be positioned about 6in (15cm) along the handles of the other two so that its head extends over the ends of theirs.

Because this top club is slightly forward, when you throw the clubs up it will make one more spin than the other two, for example, a double rather than a single spin. Catch the first two and there is still time to throw one of them in the air before catching the third and starting your routine.

If you have large hands this move can be done one-handed, holding the clubs in the same position.

Inside foot kick up

This is a trick best practised barefoot which may sound more complicated than it is. To kick up with your right foot, lift it up during the cascade and place a club on to it. The handle should be pointing to the right. Then lower the club to the floor. The foot should be turned so that it is at right angles to the floor with the club nestled against the ball of the foot. Quickly step over the club with your left foot and cross your legs by about 4in (10cm), with the left foot in front of the right to create the necessary angle. Sweep your right leg directly out to the left, the club will rise into the air and, if all goes well, it can be caught with a single spin.

CLUB ENDINGS

Double or triple throw

As mentioned earlier, when you want to finish juggling toss the club from your right hand up high. Catch the incoming club in your right hand, transfer it to your left hand and you then have your right hand free to catch the third club. This is a good ending as there is little chance of missing the last catch.

Spin round

Even with a simple catch at the end you can make it look more interesting by continuing the movement from the spin and doing a pirouette.

Dropped doubles

This ending is used by some professional jugglers who work their routine so that they end up at the front right of the stage. From there they run with doubles across the stage into the left entrance, drop all their clubs off-stage and return, possibly with a cartwheel, to take their bow.

Four clubs

This is achieved by juggling two clubs in each hand. To practise, therefore, juggle each hand singly until you can get the clubs going up and down in a smooth rhythm with single spins. The wrist action should be kept to a minimum and an even pace maintained. To stop the clubs just catch both in one hand. When you feel ready to try both hands at once your first priority is to throw them to the same height from both hands. You also need to avoid collisions.

There are a number of variations in pat-terns you can introduce to four club juggling. You can begin by throwing the clubs in an identical pattern from both hands but then switch your trajectory from one of the hands so that the two inside clubs are moving to-gether as are the two outside ones. You can also juggle while moving round in a circle and try a few double or triple spins. A further interesting variation is to start the left hand half a beat after the right so that they are both out of phase. Then the clubs are all rising at diffe-rent times and, although it is essentially the same as the simple column juggling, the movement of the clubs looks very different.

To stop four clubs you can just catch two in each hand but this is likely to lead to error. So, we suggest you throw the club from your left hand with a triple spin. Catch and hold the two right hand clubs and transfer the one in the left hand across so that the left hand is free to catch the club as it returns from the triple. For greater effect you can drop down on one knee.

5 Juggling with other objects

Juggling is a form of 'object manipulation' and there are several related skills which, while they may not be strictly classified as juggling, incorporate many similar characteristics. In this chapter we describe several of these skills which are recognised areas of a juggler's craft as well as describing juggling with objects other than balls and clubs.

Juggling with rings

Rings are normally made of plastic (ABS or polypropylene) or plywood and are approximately 1/8in (0.3cm) thick, with an outside diameter of 12-13in (30-32cm) and a grip of 1¼-1¾in (3.1-4.4cm). They are unstable in any wind and, although wider, heavier rings can be tried, they are normally of no use outside. Rings are as easy to use as balls and are preferred for juggling with more than five objects as they can be held more comfortably and, because of their narrowness, can be positioned more accurately without colliding.

However, rings can be fun just by using three. One good effect is the colour change which the rings can make while they are being juggled. To do this paint on one side of the rings or apply sticky back plastic. As you juggle change your grip between catches so that, instead of grabbing them in the normal way, your hands are turned in towards your body and your palms are facing upwards. Catch the rings on the palm and between the thumb and forefinger. Then, by bringing your hands round to throw the rings up as normal, they are flicked over so quickly that the audience cannot see how it is done.

An effective end to a rings routine is to pull them down over your head one by one as you catch them until both hands are empty.

Juggling with torches

Using torches at dusk is certain to please an audience. The combination of mesmorising spectacle with the element of danger is irresistible. Fortunately for the performer, juggling with fire is nowhere near as dangerous as it looks.

Torches are dipped in paraffin for two or three seconds with the wick totally immersed. Then the paraffin is returned to a secure and sealable container. It is important that the torches are taken to a safe place and vigorously shaken to remove excess paraffin otherwise, as you juggle, sparks of burning paraffin will flick into your face and onto the audience. It is best to soak and shake the clubs before you begin the performance as it is easy to forget in the heat of the moment!

Paraffin has a relatively low heat and flame and is not as volatile as petrol, for example. The only disadvantage is that if you are working outdoors on a windy day you may use a whole box of matches trying to light the torches. One solution is to prime one of them with a little of lighter fluid after soaking it. Before lighting the torches check the wind direction. If you are working indoors check the position of any heat detectors and let the management know what you are doing.

When the torches are lit hold them upright and away from your body. Practise a few times without lighting the wick to get the feel of them. This is good practice but, once they are lit, they will move through the air a little slower because of the drag caused by the flame. We have found that it is very rare to catch the wrong end of the club by accident but, even if you do, it is unlikely to cause you any damage as you drop it very quickly. In fact, we sometimes create tension by purposely catching the wrong end. We usually do this right at the beginning of the juggle, before the clubs have had a chance to warm up, and also give the club a low throw so it does not hit the hand with great force. However, we do not recommend trying this until you are proficient with the torches.

There are a number of tricks that are well suited to torches. One is to throw a club under a leg accompanied by a suitable facial expression. Others are overhead arcs, the helicopters, exaggerated chops, behind the back throws and double spins.

Juggling with two ping-pong balls and a bat

There is a neat little comedy routine that can be done with these. Hold the two ping-pong balls in one hand and the bat in the other. Toss one of the balls in a cascade pattern and as you throw the bat you give it a single spin. Although the balls are very light they can be caught fairly easily. To bring in a variation catch the bat and bounce the balls off it before returning to the cascade pattern. After a while you catch one of the balls in a hole in the top of your hat . . . with a quizzical look you can then produce a ball you have previously concealed in your mouth, with the implication that it has travelled through your head, and briefly continue the juggle. Alternatively you can place a little trap door in the front of the hat so that the ball goes in at the top and out at the front to continue with the routine.

Balancing a ping-pong ball on the nose

This is an easy trick which appears impossible and benefits from a good build-up in which you explain how many hours of practice it took to perfect. Explain that generally speaking the smaller and lighter an object the harder it is to balance and suggest that two members of the audience may care to attempt to balance a ping-pong ball on their noses. Not surprisingly, they will fail. Then announce that not only will you succeed in balancing a ping-pong ball, but that you intend to juggle three, toss one up high, catch it and balance it on your nose!

Your audience will be suitably impressed as you keep control of the ball, swaying your head from side to side to keep it balanced. At a suitable point in the wild applause this trick generates, bow and the ball is shown to be firmly stuck to the end of your nose!

The secret is that before starting your show you coat your nose and one of the ping pong balls with a rubber adhesive and let it dry. One such, Copydex, starts white yet dries clear and is a suitable one to use. The two ping-pong balls which the audience members use are obviously undoctored and the third is easily introduced for the juggling. The coated ball will not stick to your hands but will be identifiable after some practice and so you will know which one to toss up high during the juggle. As it makes contact with the glue on your nose it will stick firmly. It is important, though, to maintain the illusion of balance with your head kept well back and the right sort of body movements.

Cigar boxes

Although reinforced genuine cigar boxes are sometimes used, most jugglers use more sturdy ones measuring approximately 8 × 5 × 2½in (20 × 12 × 6cm). These are attractively decorated and have strips of suede or similar material glued to the ends to ensure a good, non-slip surface when they are manipulated. Three boxes are held, as in the diagram, with one hand on each outside box, pinning the middle one between them. The boxes are held comfortably about waist high with a firm grip. The object is to move one or more of the boxes and replace it before the loose box falls to the floor.

Try moving the right hand box away from the other two and quickly back again to pin the middle one before it falls to the ground. You will find that, if you do not raise the three boxes about 6in (15cm) before attempting the move, the middle one will fall before you can replace the end box. The 6in (15cm) upward movement allows you time to make a move while the boxes start to descend to the normal level. It is possible to develop a smooth, rhythmic movement which gives the illusion of the boxes being suspended in mid air. Practise all the moves you can discover with both hands. A few of the building block moves are described below.

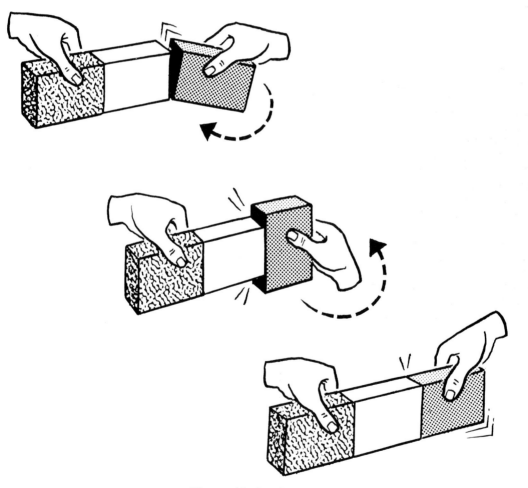

Moves with cigar boxes

END TURNS

From the basic position take the right hand box and turn it upside down before replacing it. Your right hand is now holding the box from below. Reverse the procedure to return the hand to the top.

END TURNS WITH A GRIP CHANGE

Instead of reversing the procedure, to return the hand from the bottom to the top, release the right hand altogether and bring it round and back to the top. So, instead of moving the box and the hand, you simply move your hand from the bottom to the top.

With both these moves the middle box has remained relatively still while the outside ones have been manipulated. Two basic methods of moving the middle box are called spins and take-outs.

SPINS

Here the middle box is spun a half turn and caught back in the middle. The only change is that it is upside-down. The spin is given to the box at the top of the upward 6in (15cm) movement before the boxes are released. Right-handers generally find it easier to give a counter-clockwise spin. You can also try with a complete 360° revolution, or even more than that.

TAKE-OUTS

The right hand lets go of the right outside box,

grabs the middle box and brings it very quickly round to the outside to pin the right outside box in the middle.

You can try to combine different styles of move – for example, an end turn with a spin. Several moves, such as end turns, can be done simultaneously with each hand.

BODY MOVES

From the basic position try raising one leg and removing the right hand box for long enough to bring the leg through the gap, before pinning the middle box underneath the leg. For a comical effect you can trap the leg between the middle and outside boxes.

A similar move is to put the right hand box behind the back to meet the other two. The body shape looks similar to juggling behind the back.

BALANCE MOVES

In addition to the moves involving three cigar boxes there are those based more on balance which utilise five or more boxes. One such is the nine box split and balance. Nine boxes are held as shown in the diagram with their broadest sides together. The middle box sticks up slightly and pressure is applied from the ends of the nine boxes to slide them into the position shown. Tip this gently towards the right hand and turn box 9 vertically. Hold the balance with your right hand as you remove box 1 with your left hand and place it under box 9. Lift the entire arrangement onto your chin or forehead to balance.

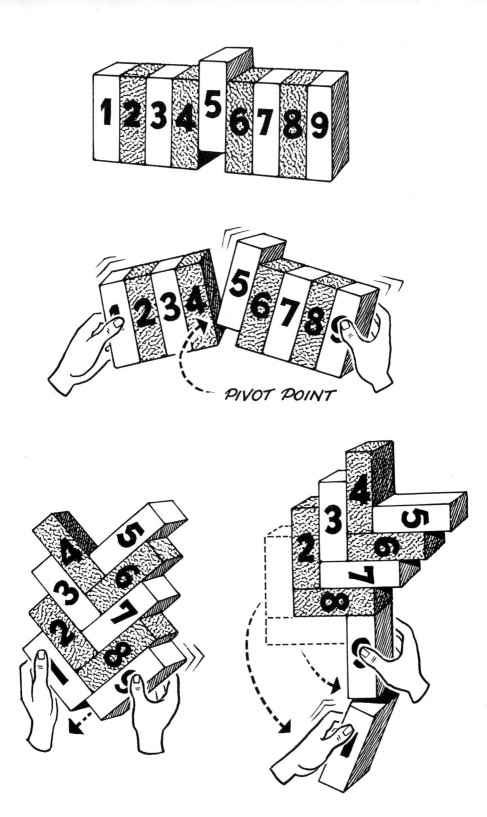

The nine box split and balance

The diabolo

This is a form of toy similar in concept to the yo-yo and spinning top. It seems to have come from China and was very popular in Britain around the turn of the century. It looks like two cones stuck together at their narrowest points and is spun on a string, then flicked into the air before being caught back on the string. Recently it has become popular amongst jugglers who have seen it used by Chinese performers. Of particular interest is a bamboo humming diabolo which, as it spins faster and faster, hums with increasing vol-

Spinning the diabolo: stage one

ume until it sounds like a space ship landing.
The majority of diabolos are made of rubber
or plastic and are most versatile if they are
fairly large and heavy.

To spin the diabolo, lay it on the ground
and place the cord underneath its waist.
Take one stick in each hand and lower the
right one until it is close to the diabolo. Raise
the left hand to take up the slack and then
raise the right hand sharply upwards. This lifts
the diabolo and imparts an anti-clockwise
spin as it moves along the cord towards the
left hand. At this point drop the right hand so
that the diabolo falls back again to the right
end of the cord. Then whip the right hand up
to spin it back again. The left hand stays practically motionless while the right one controls
the spin of the diabolo through the use of
sharp, but controlled and even, movements.
If the diabolo starts to swing round to your
right or left you need to move with it so that
you are always standing opposite its end.

You may find the diabolo tilts and is in

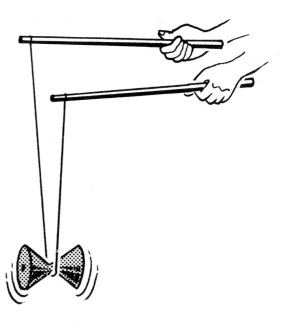

Spinning the diabolo: stage two

Catching the diabolo

danger of falling off the cord. To correct this move the left hand in the same direction as that in which the diabolo is tilting. If it tilts away from you move the left hand forwards in a horizontal plane; if it tilts towards you draw the left hand backwards. This will bring the diabolo back on to an even keel, at which point the hands can be brought level with each other again.

Before it can be tossed up the diabolo must be spinning fast enough to continue while in the air and when being caught. Otherwise it will tumble end over end and prove impossible to catch. When it is spinning bring your hands almost together and then sharply away from each other to stretch the cord taut and flick the diabolo high into the air. The motion should not be a jerk but the quicker and larger it is the higher the diabolo will rise.

It is caught at the far right end of the cord with the stick held high to help to aim the cord at the diabolo. The sticks are held well apart but, as the diabolo makes contact, the cord is slackened by bringing the sticks together. This allows the diabolo to sag into the cord rather than bounce off it. Recommence the spinning motion immediately. An alternative is to allow the diabolo to bounce off the cord without spinning it between catches. To do this, catch the diabolo on the right end of the cord and keep the cord taut, running the diabolo along it before flicking it off again.

There are many moves that can be achieved once the basics have been learnt. The diabolo can be made to climb the cord by gradually raising the left-hand stick up to head height. The diabolo will be near the right-hand stick which is used to make a loop of cord around it. As you bring the sticks apart to make the cord taut the diabolo will rise up. To work effectively the diabolo needs to be spinning quite fast initially.

You can also try passing the diabolo to a partner standing next to you.

Bouncing the diabolo

Devil sticks

These are a set of three sticks which seem to defy the laws of gravity. The two which are hand held are each about 19in (48cm) long and ½in (1.3cm) in diameter and generally encased in rubber tubing or towelling grip. The one to be manipulated is around 25-30in (63-76cm) long – 1½-2in (4-5cm) in diameter at each end but tapering to 1-1½in (2.5-4cm) in the middle. It is generally wrapped with a thin material or plastic coating and decorated.

Begin by standing the large stick vertically in front of you while holding the smaller ones in a natural grip at either side of it. Tilt the

Devil sticks

large stick until it falls and, when it reaches an angle of 45°, knock it back with one stick just above the middle. As it falls to the other side knock it back again. These movements should be as relaxed as possible. Gradually try and lift the centre stick off the floor by giving it a slight upwards, as well as sideways, knock. The outward taper of the central stick helps this. To speed up the swing also knock the central stick below the middle with the left hand stick as you knock it with the right hand stick above the middle and vice versa. You may find that there is a tendency for the central stick to roll horizontally between the other two. This is counteracted by pushing one of the hand held sticks forward until it straightens out.

Alternatively, the horizontal roll can be encouraged and one stick only used to control it as you take the left-hand one away and just strike the central stick lightly on the underside close to the middle as it comes round. The same move can be done in the vertical plane by keeping the central stick spinning with a gentle tap slightly below the centre each time it comes round towards the horizontal plane.

Balancing

This is a skill commonly used by jugglers either as a separate activity or in conjunction with juggling. For example, while juggling

THE SECRET IS TO WATCH THE TOP OF THE OBJECT

Balancing a broom

ubs, it is possible to place one very quickly c. nto the chin or nose and hold it balanced for a moment before allowing it to drop back to a hand to start the juggle off again.

We suggest you start by trying to balance a tall, top heavy object – a broom for example. Place the stick upright on the palm of your hand. Watch the top of the broom and, as it starts to topple to one side, move your hand in the same direction. This will bring the broom back to the vertical position again. It is very important to watch the top of the object being balanced and, as soon as it starts to topple, move your hand to counteract it.

Initially your hand will have to move quite a lot to keep the broom vertical but gradually you will find it easier to control the movement. Then you will be ready to try to balance shorter, lighter objects – a club, for example – on your palm or fingertip. Try to keep the movements as small as possible.

When you are confident with this you can practise with objects on your forehead, nose or chin. A tennis racquet is a useful object to start with. Tilt your head back and place it upright on your forehead, watch the top and move your head underneath in the same way as you moved your hand when balancing the broom. At first you will have to move your head a lot but gradually it becomes easier to maintain the balance, although you can never stop moving completely.

Other objects which can be balanced in-

Balancing a top hat

clude umbrellas, top-hats and chairs. With some objects you cannot see the top so you have to estimate where it is. When you become more advanced practise juggling while balancing objects on your forehead.

6 More advanced ball juggling

Juggling four balls

As with four clubs the simplest pattern is juggling two balls in each hand going up in unison. Each hand makes the inward scoop action as described in three ball columns (page 19). So, each hand can be practised singly before the use of four balls is attempted. Once the simple pattern is running smoothly you can think about introducing a few variations such as high throws, juggling each hand out of time and moving round in a circle.

It is also possible to shower four or more balls and this certainly looks effective. Most people do, however, find it more difficult than columns.

Five ball juggling

For many jugglers the ability to juggle five balls is the pinnacle of their ambition and to do this entails commitment and practice. Many have found that they have persevered despite reaching new levels of frustration.

The pattern with five balls is the same as the cascade with three except that there are always at least three balls in the air. To begin, hold three balls in your right hand and two in your left. The balls are thrown from alternate hands – right, left, right, left, right – in a cascade pattern but tossed about 1ft 6in (45cm) higher than usual. They need to be thrown out very rapidly and accurately – make sure that they all reach the same height at a point practically above the hand in which they will land.

It will take many attempts before you get the feel of using five balls. You may find it helpful to practise the three ball flash as described on page 24, clapping your hands while all three balls are in the air. The clap is replaced by the other two balls when juggling five. The first sense of achievement comes when you can see the pattern forming as you throw the five out, although you catch only one or two of them. Gradually you will learn to make one complete cycle and then to maintain a ragged pattern which becomes smoother with practice.

When you have succeeded in getting five balls in the air in a regular pattern it is possible to carry out tricks such as under the leg, the reverse cascade or even to increase the number of balls to seven or nine.

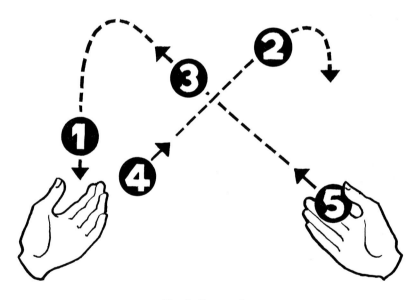

Five ball cascade

Bounce juggling

Instead of juggling upwards you might like to try juggling downwards. For this you need a smooth flat floor and very bouncy balls. As mentioned earlier, the best are silicon balls especially made for jugglers, followed closely by Canadian lacrosse balls or rubber dog balls. It is, of course, possible to do a number of bouncing tricks with ordinary tennis balls.

There are two ways of throwing a ball out of your hands. Either toss the ball gently upwards and let it drop and bounce off the floor, catching it with your palm downwards; or, keeping your hands palm downwards force the ball down and catch it as before on the rebound. The first of these is the easiest. Stand with your feet slightly apart and your weight evenly balanced between them. Start as usual with two balls in your right hand and throw them as you would in a reverse cascade. Let those from your right hand hit a point in front of your left foot and vice versa (see below).

Now force the balls down as shown in the next diagram. As you can see this is a slightly faster pattern.

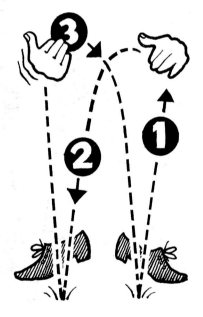

Bounce: version one – reverse cascade

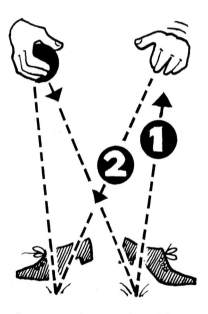

Bounce: version two – forced down

Try doing a shower, forcing the balls down with your right hand and passing those from the left hand across to your right hand (see below). It is also possible to incorporate floor bounces into a normal three ball juggle, either with all three balls or with one ball given a lot of spin which is flicked away from you and bounces back into the pattern.

Five ball bouncing is sometimes claimed to be easier than ordinary five ball juggling and it certainly requires less physical effort. Five balls can be bounced in both the reverse cascade and forcing down patterns.

The truly ambitious can go on to higher numbers and we saw Antonio Bucci perfectly bounce-juggling seven balls for 10 min at the 1985 European Juggling Convention.

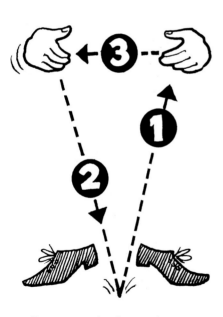

Bounce: version three – shower

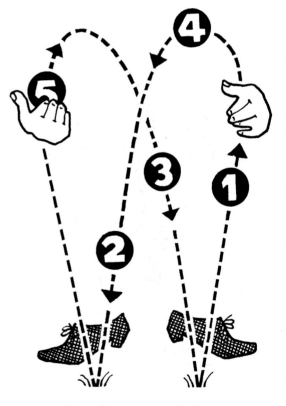

Five ball reverse cascade bounce

Head bouncing and rolling

One effective trick is to bounce a ball on your head and then cause it to skip with a small piece of rope about 2ft (65cm) long. What you need to be able to do first of all is to maintain the ball bouncing on your head in a regular pattern, about 1ft (30cm) into the air with each bounce. Hold the rope 6in (15cm) above your forehead and slightly in front of it. As you head the ball start the rope spinning so that it goes under and then over the ball as it falls down. This trick seems difficult at first but can be accomplished with practise.

After a few skips of the rope you can then let the bounces get smaller and smaller until finally you balance the ball on your forehead. It will probably help if you raise both your hands in the air to help with the balance. This is, of course, a trick that many professional footballers can do with a large ball but a small ball is, in many ways, easier.

Head bouncing and skipping

The ball can now be rolled to other places. One move is to roll it onto an ear. This is achieved by a deft flick of the head. To practise it you need to place the ball on your ear to get a feel of what it is like. It is very difficult to do this trick with long hair or sideburns. To roll onto your right ear you maintain the ball motionless on your forehead. Then you move your head to a horizontal position moving it quickly at first but then slowing down. To get the ball to roll smoothly, you will need to use your neck muscles and also bend both legs, with the right one pushed further forward. Your right hand will be raised and your left hand lowered to maintain balance. Reverse the movement to flick the ball back onto your forehead.

To roll the ball onto the back of your neck, do a smooth rolling action. The trunk of the body is moved forwards, the legs remaining firm and the arms are moved down and backwards to help form a hollow at the back of the neck into which the ball will nestle.

It is then possible to roll the ball down your back but make sure that you do not have a belt that protrudes and knocks the ball off centre. As the ball drops between your legs you can reach out with your hand and catch it for a nice end to a rolling routine.

Head bouncing and rolling the ball onto your ear

7 Juggling patterns for two people

In the same way as musicians enjoy being part of a duo, quartet or orchestra, jugglers enjoy passing objects with others to share the exhilaration of developing a hundred different patterns. As with musicians in an orchestra teamwork and a feeling for rhythm are keys to success. While it is easiest to pass with one other person there is no reason why you cannot include ten or more others.

This chapter teaches the basic structure and timing of passing when using balls. In Chapter 8 we explain club passing and more advanced moves.

Three ball juggling between two people

Many jugglers move straight from solo juggling to passing six objects without fully exploring the possibilities of manipulating three objects between two people. Although we describe the moves using balls most can also be done with clubs.

STEALING

a) From the front

The first juggler cascades three balls and the partner standing opposite reaches out and steals the balls without breaking the cascade pattern. To look effective it is important that the balls are stolen and not just passed across. The first juggler, sometimes called the gamekeeper, should be juggling slowly, keeping the hands low and tossing the balls a little higher than usual. The poacher should mentally choose a ball and grab it at its peak using the right hand. With the left hand the next ball is grabbed at its peak. The first ball is then thrown from the right hand, the third is stolen and a cascade pattern of juggling is started. The roles can then be reversed and the gamekeeper becomes the poacher.

If you are performing this trick in front of an audience it helps to make it funnier if the gamekeeper continues making a juggling action for a moment after the balls have been stolen.

With some practise the partners should be able to quickly chase each other back and forth with the poacher stealing the balls and then losing them as the roles are reversed.

POACHER GRABS THE BALL AT ITS PEAK

Stealing from the front

b) From the side

This is similar to stealing from the front, except that the gamekeeper loses the balls before noticing the poacher. The poacher approaches the gamekeeper from behind and a little to the left and slides his right hand between the gamekeeper and the balls, just above the forearms. The first ball is poached with the left hand as it peaks over the gamekeeper's left one. The right hand is already in position to steal the second and the gamekeeper throws the third ball up while moving slightly to the right and backwards, allowing the poacher to move into the central position.

The gamekeeper can now get the balls back by circling round the poacher and repeating the steal. As you become more experienced the rate of stealing can be speeded up until it seems as though the balls stay still while the jugglers rush around in circles. Audiences love to see stealing start off very slowly and gradually increase to a frenetic chase.

JUGGLER NUMBER TWO APPROACHES JUGGLER ONE FROM BEHIND LEFT

Stealing from the side

Six ball passing between two people

Before attempting to pass each partner should be able to juggle in a smooth, rhythmic cascade pattern. The participants should also be able to look through the pattern and watch other things happening instead of concentrating solely on their own props. When passing it is important that each partner is juggling at the same time; otherwise passes will not arrive at the correct time to fit into the rhythm of the cascade pattern. It is much easier to achieve an even tempo between you if you can be sure of starting to juggle simultaneously.

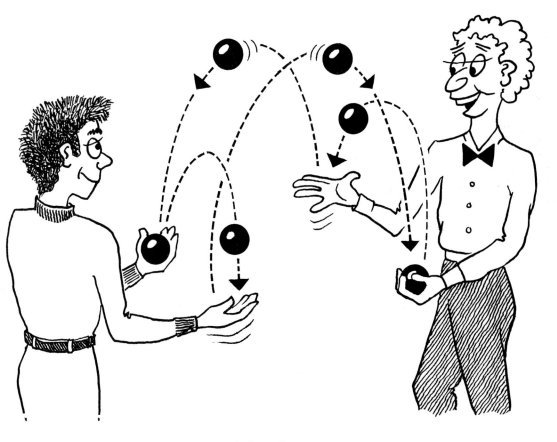

Ball passing

THE STANDARD START

Jugglers throughout the world have a standard way of starting. Each juggler has two balls in his right hand and one in his left and they stand facing each other. To signal their readiness to begin, the pre-determined starter raises both hands in the air as if being held up in a robbery. The other follows and both bring their hands down together. They start the same moves at the same time and are, therefore, juggling in unison. If they slip up on their timing and bring their hands down at different times they cannot juggle in tempo and should begin the opening sequence again.

JUGGLING IN RHYTHM AND WHEN TO PASS

Once you and your partner have started together you begin counting each ball as it leaves your *right* hand. Try and match the speed of your juggling with that of your partner so that you are counting in unison. Try also to watch your partner's pattern while juggling. As important as starting and juggling in unison is passing at the same time. It is usual to start off by passing the third ball to leave the right hand and it is best to count *down* to the pass:

TWO First throw from *right* hand to self (starting to juggle)
ONE Second throw from *right* hand to self
PASS Third throw from *right* hand to your partner.

If you both inexperienced at passing it could be helpful at the start for one person only to juggle while the other just catches the ball as it is passed to their left hand. It is important to make the throw as accurate as possible – it should go in a straight line from your right hand to your partner's left one and should go just outside the line of your partner's body. Most people find it best to place their left foot slightly forward as this helps to ensure that the line of the pass is correct.

At first you should end up with one ball in each hand and your partner should have the third. To continue, your partner passes the ball from the left hand to the right and then tosses it to your left hand for you to continue. As the third ball approaches you make room for it by tossing the ball currently in your left hand to your right one and start juggling

again. After you have worked this out you can progress by your partner holding a ball in the right hand and throwing it to your left hand at the same time as you make the pass.

When each partner feels confident about the standard start and the accuracy of their throws they can attempt to pass six balls. Throw the ball from your right hand to your partner's right hand to your left one and both you and your partner keep the cascade pattern going. Set up a rhythm and both count each ball as it leaves the right hand (two, one, pass; two, one, pass). This is known as thirds since you are passing every third ball from your right hand.

SPEEDING UP THE RATE OF PASSING

Whether you will be passing the third, second or every ball it is normal to make the first throw with the third ball. To progress, you can try passing every second ball instead of every third. So, from the start the rhythm would be: two, one, pass; one, pass; one, pass. Thus, apart from the start, you are passing every other ball.

Once you have mastered passing every other ball it is logical to try passing every time. You begin, as always, with the standard start and the rhythm goes: two, one, pass; pass; pass. This is referred to as passing solids or showering.

THREE THREE TEN

This is a spectacular way of increasing the speed of passing which is both enjoyable for jugglers and very effective when performed before an audience. The gradual building of the frequency of passes has the effect of making the final throws seem twice as fast as they are to a lay audience.

The three three ten is made up as follows: three thirds (two, one pass; two, one, pass; two, one, pass), three passes with every other ball (one, pass; one, pass; one, pass) and ten solids (pass; pass; pass; pass; pass; pass; pass; pass; pass; pass).

LEFT TO RIGHT HAND PASSING

This is effectively the same as ordinary passing except that you start with two balls in your left hand and count the balls as they leave it. Try to build up to a three three ten. Also try passing first from your right hand and then from your left hand on every other timing. You will find you pass the ball you catch straight back from the hand you caught it in.

RECOVERING DROPS WHEN PASSING

It is not necessary to stop juggling or break the rhythm of passing if one partner drops one of the balls. To practise the pick-up while still juggling try on thirds, initially, dropping a ball (or possibly a beanbag as it will not roll away) by your right foot. Stop juggling and hold one ball in each hand until your partner, under normal rhythm, passes to you. You then have three balls and your partner stops juggling until you make the pass across. Immediately after passing pick up the ball with your right hand and throw it across at the same time as your partner passes to you on normal thirds timing.

Throughout this sequence passes will have been made on thirds timing and if the pick-up is skilful it will appear to an audience that the drop was intentional.

The same principle is followed on every other passing, although there is obviously less time to make a pick-up before a ball is passed to you.

When passing solids it is extremely difficult to pick up a drop. Again practice dropping an object but keep juggling as if all six are there. In other words, maintain the timing by keeping a gap where the missing prop should be. Follow the gap around the four hands, waving the empty hand that would hold the dropped object. You will notice that the gap moves from your partner's right hand to your left one and then to your right one. The pick-up is made in the split second when a gap, instead of an object, is in the hand nearest the dropped object. This is, of course, very difficult to do and it takes a long time to be able to make smooth pick-ups while passing solids, but it looks and feels great once you have the knack.

If an article falls halfway between partners, a long way behind or to one side then, instead of one juggler darting to get it, both should move so that the partner who is to pick it up is standing right by the object, while still passing, and therefore has more time to pick-up and pass accurately.

8 Club passing

The basic timing and manoeuvres for passing clubs are the same as for balls. It is important that both jugglers are competent with the clubs since the need for accurate throws is more important than with balls because of the clubs' increased size and weight. Accuracy is also helped if the correct way of throwing is used.

The right hand holding the club to be passed should be brought down until it is by your leg and then your arm should be thrown forward, with the hand letting go of the club when the arm is almost at full extension in front of you. The throw is almost totally an arm action with a minimal amount of wrist movement. Too much wrist creates a short, fast spin which is difficult both to control and catch. The club should make one revolution and be caught by your partner's left hand with the handle pointing down. This catch should take place in line with but a little to the side of your partner's left shoulder.

If each of the jugglers concentrates on the accuracy of their throws the catching should be made much easier. However, if one of the throws comes at unusual speed or angle then it may be difficult to recover and the next throw could be even worse. Once the first club is caught, the arm is brought down in an outside sweep and the club is thrown in a usual cascade pattern.

As mentioned in the previous chapter most jugglers find it helpful to place the left foot forward to counteract the tendency for the club that is passed to swing in towards their partner's body. As with balls you should attempt to progress from thirds through every other to solids and then to a three three ten sequence.

From this point there are two logical areas of progression which can ultimately be combined. These are to add trick throws to the basic pattern and to pass in groups of three or more.

Trick throws while passing

Many trick throws are best explained in the context of every other passing, although all can be done on thirds and most, after a lot of practice, on solids.

DOUBLE SPIN

This is one of the easiest tricks which is good visually and is also a very useful building block for others. The club being passed rises higher than usual and makes two revolutions before landing in your partner's hand. The important thing about the trick is that the club is thrown early and from the left hand to your partner's left hand. To allow time for the double spin and the greater height the club must be thrown half a beat earlier than usual. This is achieved by throwing the club directly from your left hand to your partner's left hand which means that your right hand is totally by-passed. So, if you are throwing a double in every other timing, the club that is passed to your left hand is thrown back immediately with a double spin to the partner's left hand.

If the passed club is thrown correctly and in an unhurried manner it will arrive at your partner's hand at the same time and in the same way as usual and the rhythm is maintained. However, the juggler who throws the double must resist the temptation to throw the next club that arrives in the right hand as it would be out of time, and so stops juggling for a very short time.

THE TRIPLE SPIN

This is similar in concept to the double spin. However the club being passed goes even

The double spin pass

higher and takes longer to arrive. The club is thrown from the right hand but one beat earlier than usual. On every other timing the club that makes the triple spin is thrown immediately after the previous pass from the right hand. Having thrown the triple you are left with one club in each hand for a moment and must wait to resume the normal pattern until your partner has passed a club to you and you have passed one club from your left to your right hand. So the right hand count from the start is:

Two, one, pass; one, pass; one, pass; triple pass; pause, one, pass.

The triple spin throw should, as with other throws, be basically an arm action and, therefore, high and graceful. If all goes well it is caught in the normal way by your partner who then maintains the regular 'every other' rhythm.

During the gap after you have thrown the triple you may find time to crouch down and knock your clubs on the floor a couple of times before catching your partner's pass. Alternatively you might like to try and do a rapid pirouette.

You need not return to a conventional pass after the triple. You might like to try instead to pass a series of triples with a self pass in between. The triples tend to become increasingly erratic, however, and you should desist if your partner shows signs of shell shock!

DOUBLE AND TRIPLE SPIN THROWS

A fast flurry of tricks is achieved by throwing, on every other timing, a normal pass followed immediately by a double from the left hand and immediately again by a triple from the right. Although each throw follows immediately from the other, avoid increasing the pace from the usual rhythm and attempt to maintain accuracy.

UNDER THE LEG THROWS

If, while juggling along, you can throw a club from your right hand under your leg to your left hand it just takes a little redirection of the throw to pass the club to a partner. It helps accuracy if you turn to your right so that your leg is parallel with your partner. If you are feeling adventurous you might like to try passing alternately from under the right leg (the outside of it) and from under your left leg (the inside of it). You can also try a self pass under one leg in between passes. In passing in this way you may find it helpful to hold the club nearer the knob than usual, but try to avoid too much wrist action and overspin.

BEHIND THE BACK THROWS

It is best if this is first attempted while only one partner is juggling as the club often flies towards the catcher's face while learning the move. As in the under the leg throws turn towards the right and push your hips forward, then quickly pass the club behind your back to your partner and let your right hand catch the club from your left as usual. The need for speed and accuracy makes this move tricky enough, but it is also complicated by the risk of the incoming club being hit by yours if you have not passed near enough to your body and in an accurate line to your partner's left hand.

THE CHEATS PIROUETTE

Instead of risking life and limb pirouetting after having thrown a triple just make a normal pass, stop juggling and catch the incoming club in your arms while holding the other two. Pirouette while sorting out the clubs so you have two in your right hand and one in your left and then pass one club out, as the other one comes in, to start your juggling again.

THE RIGHT TO RIGHT HAND DOUBLE

Instead of throwing a single to your partner's left hand throw a double spin from your right hand to your partner's right hand. It will arrive just at the right time to be returned to you.

THE LEFT TO RIGHT HAND TRIPLE

As a club arrives in your left hand throw it straight back again from the left hand as a high triple to your partner's right hand.

ONE PERSON IN THE MIDDLE

This is a popular stage item. For this trick two jugglers pass clubs either side of a volunteer, or victim, who stands in between them. The person in the middle should stand completely still with their hands by their sides.

Also, someone can walk through the gap between two jugglers just after they have passed. Try this on thirds first, and then on every other timing. Obviously tricks thrown out of sequence such as doubles cannot be used.

THE MOUTH KNOCKOUT

When two partners are adept at passing either side of the volunteer they can attempt to knock an object, such as a bar of chocolate, out of their mouth. It should be held loosely between moistened lips and not gripped by the teeth.

The juggler who is to do the knockout should start off passing wide and then gradually home in, always erring on the cautious side. To practise it is sometimes best to use a long straw.

When performing this on stage some performers like to test the volunteer's nerve and ability to stay still. They signal to each other that they are ready to begin with arms held high. They then take a step towards the volunteer and sweep the clubs down, without letting go, either side of his face while screaming. If the volunteer survives this the knock-out will present no problems!

BACK TO BACK CLUB PASSING

Two jugglers standing back to back can each pass clubs over their right shoulders with one and a half spin throws. The clubs are caught with the left hand in a similar position to the usual passing catch. To signal the start the lead juggler taps the other's clubs and the timing of throws is as normal. As neither of the partners can see where their throws are going there is a tendency initially to throw them too far so as to avoid hitting their partner. In this position it is necessary for the jugglers to talk continuously to each other so that the throws can be altered and accuracy improved.

Passing with two or more people (formation juggling)

Many of these formations are explained with three jugglers involved. Further on we explain how to expand the formation for more jugglers.

THE FEED

One juggler (the feeder) passes clubs first to juggler A and then juggler B. To an onlooker it seems that all three are passing at the same time. The ideal is for the feeder to throw solids and for A and B to throw every others. However, it is easier to learn the pattern with the feeder passing every other club and A and B passing every fourth club from their right hand (fourths).

To begin, all three partners start simultaneously in the standard way and the feeder makes the first pass with A on thirds timing. From then on A passes every fourth club. Juggler B's first pass is the fifth club from the right hand. This corresponds with the feeder's second every other pass and from then on juggler B also passes on fourths.

It is important that both A and B try to make their throws to the feeder as accurate as possible and at the right time. If any of the three jugglers gets off the tempo there is a possibility that both A and B could pass to the feeder at the same time.

Once the trio have succeeded with the feeder passing every other then they can try with the feeder passing solids. Again the first pass from the feeder is on thirds timing after which A passes on every other. B's first pass is on fourths and from then on is every other.

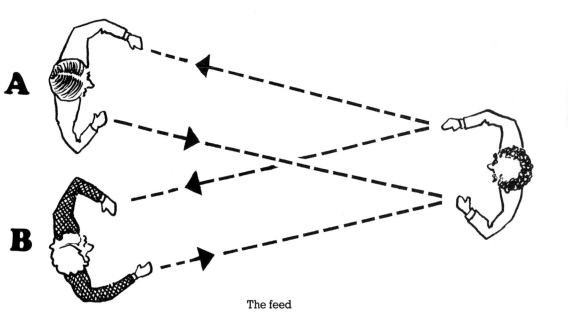

The feed

THE TRIANGLE

For these movements each juggler stands at a corner of an equilateral triangle. There are three variations we will describe in this section.

Pattern one – inside
Each juggler passes at the same time, initially on thirds, to the left hand of the partner on their left. Because the clubs pass in front of the recipient's bodies while they in turn are facing the juggler they have passed to, accuracy is of paramount importance. If the partners are mistrustful of one another then there is a danger that they may not be fully attentive to their throws. However, once the passes are smooth and regular the catches become easy and the formation flows.

Pattern two – outside
Each partner passes at the same time, initially on thirds, to the left hand of the partner on their right. The clubs are not travelling very far and should therefore be thrown gently as well as accurately.

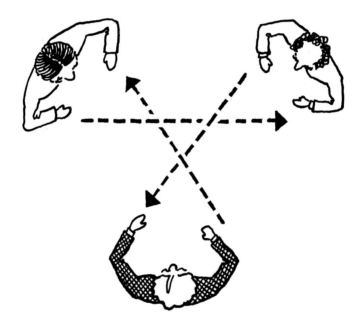

The triangle: inside

Pattern three – inside outside

The above two patterns are combined so that, having made one pass to the partner on your left, the next one goes to the one on your right.

If you are adventurous you can try building up to a three three ten with each of these patterns and also attempt other variations, such as three passes with each pattern. The same tricks can be performed with more than three people as well.

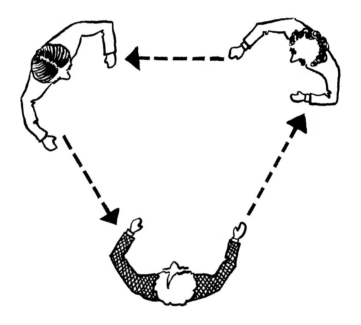

The triangle: outside

THE BOX

The box is one of the more difficult patterns to get right but it is also one of the most exhilarating. Four people are involved, each standing at the corner of an imaginary square. They face the juggler diagonally opposite to them and this is the person to whom they will pass. It is clear that if all four pass at the same time the clubs are likely to collide. In order to avoid this the teams have a staggered start. One starts a half beat before the other and passes slightly before it. There are two ways of achieving a staggered start:

1 One team starts off with two clubs in their left hands and one in their right. Both teams begin together but, for one team, the first self throw is from the left hand. The pass, which as usual is the third club to leave the right hand, is later than normal and therefore fits in between the other team's passes.

2 One team starts with arms lowered and brings their hands up as the other team brings their hands down to begin.

Each pair of jugglers can attempt to do a three-three-ten and the second team to pass should try and make their throw follow that of the first team as quickly as possible.

An alternative is for both teams to pass at the same time but for one pair to throw constant high and straight doubles over the normal passes of the other.

Finally, it is possible for all four jugglers to pass at the same time with the clubs seemingly ducking and weaving amongst each other. The key to this is for each person to juggle with widespread arms and make their passes as wide as possible. For this to succeed each juggler must be in tempo and stand exactly on the corner of the imaginary square. This results in a large central area where the clubs are passing. It is important to look out for erratically flying clubs as there are bound to be many collisions at first but, with practice, this is very effective.

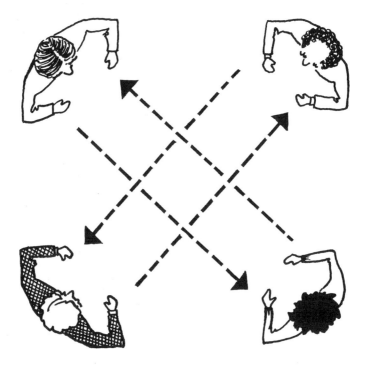

Club passing: the box

9 Getting an act together

Some people prefer to juggle purely for their own satisfaction. However, juggling is good to watch and so there are opportunities for jugglers to work out an act and perform it publicly. Both of us have wide experience in performing, both for adult audiences and for children.

It is important to become a competent juggler before you begin thinking seriously about giving shows, although if there are children in the neighbourhood they will probably like whatever you do. One of the big differences between practising juggling and performing is that when you practise you are usually pushing yourself to the limits of your ability while within a show you are aiming to entertain. This entails concentrating on the moves and tricks you know really well and have rehearsed as near to perfection as you can. You are also aiming to introduce as much variety as possible to keep the attention of the audience.

General points to remember

1 Be well prepared. Have your act well worked out beforehand and be very clear as to what you are going to do next. This will give you confidence.

2 Smile and be friendly. You will, of course, be a little nervous until you have done a few performances but the main purpose is to have fun and to help the audience have a good time.

3 When developing a juggling routine for a show it is a good idea to get the moves in a sequence so that you know exactly where you are.

Straight cabaret

In some of the larger venues your time on stage is likely to be very short – even as little as 6 min. To perform well in this kind of situation you need a tightly scheduled act, with a few spectacular tricks leading up to a big finish.

Johnny and Suma Lamonte, a brother and sister act, were probably Britain's most successful jugglers in the 1950s and 1960s. They had a totally visual act and played at all of Britain's top venues. Suma suggested that there were several key points to remember.

First of all, practise to get your act right and make sure you are as prepared as possible. Make sure that the act flows from one item to another without awkward breaks or hesitation. An act needs a good opening to capture attention, then an interesting middle which leads up to a big finish. If a good trick is performed make sure that you take the applause and allow the audience an opportunity to show its appreciation. Presentation and polish are also important and the act should be well dressed with the members being well coordinated. In their act the Lamonte's made a great deal of use of music to accentuate their tricks. At the end they juggled faster and faster in time with the music and finished by jumping off a table as the music built to a climax. Suma also stressed that the personality of the juggler is very important although she suggested that this is the one thing that cannot be easily learned.

One idea that works well for straight cabaret, but can be adapted for other audiences too, is that of the running gag. One such routine is used by Richard Chamberlin and works for adults or children. He talks throughout and keeps pretending to juggle clubs. His act runs along these lines: 'Would you like to see some juggling?' 'Yes, well so would I' 'Who's going to do it?' 'You want me to juggle?' At this point he picks up his clubs but then puts them down. He then gets one ball and tosses it from hand to hand pretending that he is doing something difficult. He picks up a second ball, passes it and then says he can do it backwards. He then turns round to show his back to the audience.

On picking up a third ball he does a few fake moves holding on to the ball and then makes comments such as 'I must admit it I was absent on the day we learned to juggle. I have friends who can juggle. I should have brought them along. One of them can do this'. He then does a juggling trick such as a cascade behind his back and says: 'But I can't do that. Watch what happens when I try'. He then tries it again and drops the balls, but says 'I have a friend who can do this'. He then goes into a little routine with shower, knee bounce, back of hand catch and then says 'But I never learnt it'. At this point any children in the audience shout that Chamberlin just did it but he replies 'You don't understand, I am only showing you what a friend can do. If I knew how to juggle I'd really do the tricks for you.'

He jokingly suggests that he will juggle three balls, toss one high in the air and catch it in his teeth but then says: 'How about a different trick – a head bounce?' Then, for the second time, he picks up the clubs but changes his mind.

After more jokes he picks up the clubs for a third time and motions to juggle them but puts them down and picks up scarves saying: 'See how fast your hands have to move to catch these razor sharp scarves'. He then juggles them with very slow hand movements.

Chamberlin next picks up the clubs for the fourth time and announces: 'And now what you've all been waiting for. I guess you'd like to see them all in the air together.' He then throws them up all together and catches them and says: 'That's not it. Here we go'. At this point he finally begins to juggle but says that he does not know how to stop. So he bangs himself on the head with one of the clubs and drops the others. Throughout the act the continued return to the clubs is used to create a great sense of anticipation.

Talking or singing while juggling

A number of people have developed talking routines or songs which they fit into their act. One which has worked successfully is an explanation of why the juggler should be leading the country. The speech is made while juggling three tennis balls and the text is as follows:

Ladies and gentlemen I think it is time that we had a new approach to politics and that you should make me prime minister (president). I promise you that if you elect me I shall not do anything *behind your back*: in fact I shall make sure my policies are well *up front*. They will not be *up in the air* but rather very much *on the ground*. You will not catch me *kneeling* in front of anyone and you can be sure I will not be *lying down* on the job. I will keep the country on the *right lines* and I promise you I will *stand* up for the rights of the poor and oppressed.

The current leaders do not know whether they are *coming or going* and some would even say that they are *off their heads*. However, you can be sure that when I am elected they will *catch it in the neck*.

There are those who would like to to be on the *straight and narrow* but you and I know there is a need for the occasional *knees up* and to bring some *bounce* into our lives. We should have fun and make sure that we go *skipping along*.

When I am elected I promise you that I will keep a *balance between right and left* and that those who need it will always *have my ear*. For too long it has been the *blind leading the blind* but I will make sure I *keep an eye on things*. When you only had other politicians it was often a *toss up* as to who to vote for but now vote for me and we will *move forward* together.

All the tricks needed for this routine are described in the book but if you find you cannot do all of them you can always substitute. The cues for the routine are as follows:

Catch it in the neck

Words in the speech	**Actions**
behind your back	toss ball behind your back
up front	shower
up in the air	high juggling
on the ground	bounce the balls
kneeling	kneel
lying down	lay down flat
right lines	train rolling
stand	stand
coming and going	toss balls over head
off their heads	head balls continuously
catch it in the neck	neck catch
straight and narrow	columns
knees up	knee bounce
bounce	head single ball
skipping along	skip with bouncing ball
balance between right and left	balance ball on forehead
have my ear	ear catch
blind leading the blind	put on a one-eyed blindfold
keep an eye on things	turn to show hole in blindfold
toss up	high throws from shower
move forward together	walk forwards and finish

It is also possible to sing while juggling. While working a summer season at Thorpe Park Colin developed a short singing routine to the tune of 'Tea for Two'.

Toss a ball into the air
It goes up without a care
It goes up I cannot stop it
When it comes down I hope I don't drop it.

Now I'm getting a little bit bolder
I'll toss the ball right over my shoulder
Juggling is fun as everyone can see.

Juggling can be faster or else be much slower
I can do it higher and then go much lower
We can play – so have a good time today.

Others have developed different songs and it clearly is an area where there is scope for much inventiveness.

Alternative cabaret

In recent years there has been a growth in the alternative cabaret circuit and juggling has been a very popular part of it. An act needs to work for about 20–30 min and it will not have professional musicians backing it. Parts of the straight cabaret circuit are very sexist, even some magic clubs do not yet allow women. However, the alternative cabaret circuit and the linked student venues are neither sexist nor racist. They also show great scope for audience participation. Charlie has experience of this kind of work as one half of a juggling duo 'The Long and the Short of It' and one of their acts is entitled the 'Breton Brothers restaurant'.

The act fits juggling into the ambience of a restaurant. Charlie juggles with three French onions which his partner Olly steals. They then go into a fast stealing routine which they call the 'Three onion run around'.

Olly then announces that Charlie will show his new trick of juggling five onions which he does for a while before dropping them and being chased to the kitchen. Olly then finds a volunteer from the audience as the first customer. He displays balancing tricks with plates and then juggles two apples and a sharp knife before ending up by catching the apple on the knife

Before leaving the stage the customer starts a race between Olly and Charlie to see who can eat an apple the faster, while juggling.

At the end of the race Charlie throws Olly the objects with which they have been juggling and Olly throws out clubs. They then pass six clubs between them before getting another volunteer from the audience. They say that they are going to juggle six clubs either side of the person but then they decide to get six knives instead. One of them mentions juggling knives either side of the volunteer to create the impression they are about to pass them close by. However, they juggle separately in cascade and indicate it was a joke. They then give the volunteer a final, unlit, cigarette and, making a joke about how they are bad for the health, knock it out of the mouth in a six club pass. Ten volunteers are then chosen to spin plastic plates. Few of the volunteers can do it the first time but they end up with the plates spinning on all the sticks for the finish of this section. The act then closes with torch juggling and passing to each other.

Entertaining children

Regular work in this area falls into a number of categories. There are shows for firms and organisations, children's birthday parties and those held in special children's theatres or youth clubs. The kind of performance you want to give obviously depends on the audience but there are a number of general principles. First of all, children like to be involved by shouting and appearing on stage to a greater degree than adults, so it is good to work routines into your act that will give the children an opportunity to join in. Secondly, children like a great deal of variety and so it is worthwhile considering activities other than juggling such as magic, singing action songs, balloon modelling, puppets and animal costumes.

One trick that works well with children is spinning specially formed plastic plates on a stick. By using five sticks and giving them to children up on the stage, there is a great deal of audience involvement. If you are performing a school Christmas show, for example, it is often a good idea to get a few children up on the stage and then encourage them to call for one of their teachers. After a while, when the plates are falling all over the place the juggler gets each person to hold the stick and places a spinning plate on each so they all spin together as a finale. A second simple trick that is good for audience participation is one with a full glass of water. The glass is placed on the forehead, the performer lies down flat and then stands up while getting the audience to clap rhythmically. It is important, though, to use an unbreakable glass. Other routines described earlier that work well with children are the egg trick, heading the wooden ball and catching the table tennis ball on the nose.

A good routine that children love is that of the 'naughty ball'. When Colin does this he uses two tennis balls of the usual colour plus one that is pink. He begins by telling the children that the pink ball is often naughty and jumps all over the place. He looks at the ball and tells it to behave itself today. After a few circuits of the cascade the pink ball shoots out to the side to be caught with great apparent difficulty, often causing Colin to crash into a wall. It then goes over his head, hits the ceiling while trying to wake someone who is having a nap upstairs, jumps into the audience, and then is caught on the back of the neck. Colin pretends he does not know where it has gone and asks the children. They shout out and he turns round to look for it. After a suitable time with this interplay he flicks the ball up and throws it into the box in disgrace.

Colin also developed a forgetful clown character which works very well. He says he is feeling very forgetful today for he had a special trick which he wanted to show the children but now he cannot remember what it was. However, while he is trying to remember it he will do another one. He then juggles with three clubs, goes across the room and drops them all, but comes back motioning as if he were still juggling. The children shout out, the juggling continues with his dropping them again in a second place and the children remind him once more. He then says: 'I must be careful or I might drop them on my toe'. This he does and the routine ends with him hopping round holding his foot and falling over.

Later in the act the forgetting routine can be used for tossing a clown's hat. The entertainer says that he is going to toss the hat into the air and catch it on his head. He tosses the hat in the air, misses it and then takes his applause as if he had completed it. The second time the catch is tried the clown trips and falls over, before completing the trick on the third occasion.

Another trick Colin tries on a regular basis for children is to say he is going to balance a chair on his chin or forehead. After much falling over the chair, sitting on it, toppling over backwards and such like, he then tries to balance it. The first time, however, he holds on with his right hand until everyone notices. The second time he lets go with his right hand but holds on with the left, until finally completing the trick on the third occasion.

On returning to the forgetful clown idea later in your act you can ask: 'Would you like to see some juggling with four clubs?' Colour the clubs so you have one each of red, yellow, blue and white. As the juggling starts you throw the white one over your shoulder or

STARTING
THE SPIN

SECTIONAL VIEW
OF THE SPECIAL PLATE

Plate spinning

drop it and juggle with the other three while saying 'Isn't this clever juggling with four?' You will find that the children notice and may well rush to pick the club up for you. Then say: 'I haven't dropped the red one' and the second time drop the yellow one. The third time you drop the blue one and again say 'I haven't dropped the red one'. So, finally, the children will know you are about to drop the red one which you then do, amidst the noise, before finally juggling all four.

THEATRE JUGGLING

There are a number of children's theatres where the routines are worked into a story. In one such juggling was used to keep away the evil monster. Every time the monster appeared juggling was used to remove its power and scare it off. In a second play *Peacemaker* by David Holman, two groups of people had quarrelled with each other. As 'reds' and 'blues' they were separated by a wall in the middle of the stage. Juggling was central to the story as it was one of the things that brought the groups together.

Another play which Colin performs successfully with a magical clown, Tricky Vickie, is called The Clown That Lost His Bounce. In this the simple plot is that Colin, the forgetful clown, will lose his ability to juggle if he loses his hat. After much juggling, singing, audience participation and magic Vickie changes from her clown costume into that of Cackling Carlos. Colin inevitably forgets his hat and Cackling Carlos finds it and steals it. Colin returns to find that he cannot juggle now. He goes to look for Vickie who appears on the other side of stage asking for Colin and there is a little run around until they meet and Vickie brings the hat back. Then Colin returns and they go into a big finish juggling on a drum and getting everyone to join in and sing.

10 Party tricks

There are various occasions when a juggler may arrive at a party or a bar and find that there is a need, or at least an opportunity, to liven everyone up a little. There are various tricks and stunts that can be done with every day objects and we include a selection here.

Juggling with beer, wine or champagne bottles

It is a simple matter to juggle with empty wine bottles as they are of a reasonable size and weight and, once you can juggle clubs fairly well, it should be easy to use wine bottles. A few tricks can be added, such as double spins, behind the back and under the leg throws. Champagne bottles are heavier but feel right and you can pretend that their weight is even greater. Small beer bottles are readily available in pubs and in addition to juggling with them you should be able to balance three on top of each other on the chin. The first is placed upside down and the next two the right way up. You can even place a lighted piece of paper in the top one for a more spectacular effect.

Balancing a chair or table on your chin

This is one of those tricks that looks much more difficult than it is in practice. Quite heavy tables can be balanced and it is good in a party situation to make sure people realise the weight. In reality, of course, you can take a great deal of weight on your chin or forehead.

Balancing bottles on your chin

Three tricks with a glass of beer or cider

The first of these is to balance a glass of beer or cider on your head, lie down and then stand up. About one in three adults will be successful at this with coaching from the juggler. A second stunt is to take a pint of beer and place it on a matchbox or pack of cards and explain that you are going to remove the box without touching the glass. The box is given a sharp hit and it is best to have a few practices at home before trying the trick in public. It is important to make sure that the table top, the bottom of the glass and the matchbox are all dry. The very nature of the trick leads to a great deal of attention and tension can be built up by a couple of false moves. However, it is not difficult to do as long as you do not lose courage at the last minute and give a weak hit. For a third stunt you need to be able to stand on your head. Explain that you can make beer travel uphill. Then, stand on your head and get someone to give you your drink. The actual drinking takes a little practice but if you have a good assistant it can be done easily enough.

Hitting a matchbox from under a glass of beer

Eggs into a glass

This is a stunt which is quite effective but takes a little organisation. Place four half pint mugs with fairly wide tops on the table and half fill them with water. Then, on top of these, place a metal baking tray, possibly making comments about the fact you have been cooking today. The tray is placed so that the part of it nearest to the right hand is, overhanging the glasses. On top of the tray, and over the glasses, place four hair rollers, making jokes about your hair. On top of these rollers put four eggs. When you pick up the eggs you can ask if anyone believes that they are not real and whether they want to catch one. If the conditions are right you can end up tossing eggs around a room. As you put each one on the rollers make an appropriate comment, such as: 'This is a really eggciting trick', 'In fact you could say it was eggcilerating', 'You must do this eggsactly right'.

Then, when all the eggs are in position, you are ready to knock the tray away and cause all the eggs to fall into the glasses. A sharp hit is needed and it is important not to follow through with the hand or you may hit the eggs and find that they go all over the floor. The tray tends to travel a good way and so in a small room it is important to move people out of the line of fire. This is not a difficult stunt to perform and is good fun. You can tease the audience a little by making one or two false hits. One way of doing it is to ask the audience to count 'One, two, three'. Then as your hand is about to knock the tray away say 'Now this is a very difficult trick so I will need some good applause. Let's have a little practice'. The audience starts to clap and you could say 'Not too much, just in case it goes wrong'. Then knock the tray away and invariably all the eggs fall. Immediately hold up the glasses so that everyone can see the eggs in position.

The important thing with this trick is to make sure that the eggs are over the glasses by looking at them in both directions. Some people use a piece of perspex for their tray

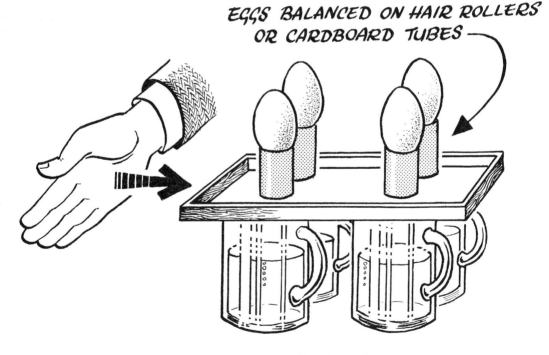

EGGS BALANCED ON HAIR ROLLERS OR CARDBOARD TUBES —

Eggs into a glass

and this has the advantage that the tops of the glasses can be seen and there is less likelihood of the eggs missing them. After a few performances the tray may get bent and so it is important to check it periodically to make sure it is square, or the eggs may topple over. Performing this trick on some stages can be made difficult because they are slightly tilted towards the audience and so the eggs are more inclined to fall. After a performance it is important to check the eggs for cracks as they can cause a great deal of mess otherwise.

Tie juggling

This trick was described in *The Juggling Bulletin* of 1950 and we have found that the effect is very amusing. As long as you can juggle with three balls you should be able to work out a tie routine. At the base of most ties there is a little pocket made from the lining. Open this up and place a ball or other object in it. By using two balls and the end of your tie you can certainly liven up a dull party as people try to overcome their surprise. We have found it possible to do most three ball juggling tricks, including heading the ball

and catching it on the back of the neck.

It is possible to use an ordinary tie for this trick, making the main part as long as possible. However, the original magazine article recommended sewing two old ties of the same colour together to give double the length. This is, of course, less natural but can lend itself to other tricks. For example, you can toss the tie backwards over the head and pretend not to notice, and continue juggling with two balls. Suddenly you notice that there is a ball missing and so look on the floor and in the air. By spinning round a complete revolution on one heel the ball will follow and come to hand so that you can continue the cascade. If you drop the end of the tie on the floor you can give it a kick with the side of your foot so that it swings up in the air. You can also surprise an audience by throwing the ball at them and jerking it back into a cascade pattern at the last moment.

The Jugglers Bulletin suggested that the funniest of all the moves is the kidney swing. The tie ball is thrown away from the body as high and far as possible and the legs are slightly bowed to allow the ball to pass between them. At this point the male juggler may give a slight squeal to add to the humour. The ball swings back and comes to hand. Other possibilities can be thought of, such as a mock strangulation as the tie gets wrapped around the neck.

Striking a match in the air

A matchbox is thrown from the right hand. While it is in the air it is struck by a match held in the same hand. The match lights and the box is caught in the other hand. The older books which described this trick suggest gluing sandpaper on to the box so that the match lights wherever the box is struck.

However, we have found that by using a jumbo-sized matchbox containing 300 matches there is no need for any preparation whatsoever. The match is held in the thumb and first finger and the other three fingers hold the box. As the box is thrown its spin is kept to a minimum and, while it is momentarily stationary at the top of its orbit, the match is struck vigorously against the side. The larger box is more easily caught than a small one and has the advantage that the match can be hidden behind it at the beginning and so the element of surprise increased.

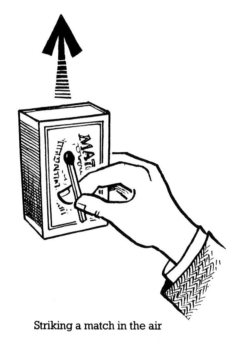

Striking a match in the air

11 Where do we go from here?

We have attempted to cover a wide range of skills in this book – from basic juggling techniques to complicated passing and from juggling for recreation to juggling in performance.

You will probably meet other jugglers and also people who would like to learn. There are already many clubs and workshops for jugglers throughout the world. For details of these the best sources are other jugglers, local theatre groups and *Kascade* magazine. For details write to Kaskade, Annastr. 7 W-6200 Wiesbaden, Germany.

Another juggling magazine called *Jugglers World* is published by the International Jugglers Association (IJA). This was formed in 1947 in America and now has over 2,500 members. It hosts an annual convention in America with over 500 people attending from top professionals to beginners. For further details of the IJA write to Box 29, Kenmore, New York 14217, USA.

Europe has several juggling conventions with one major one in September which is held in a different place each year. In addition there is one in Scandinavia and a further one in Covent Garden in the spring. These conventions are great fun and Charlie received a misdirected letter from Brigitte, a Brussels resident who described what it was like when the jugglers hit town. Her letter, published in *Kascade,* read in part:

The convention started on Thursday, although the Balls-Up Jugglers from Cardiff, England, arrived on Wednesday – living up to their name, I guess. By 11am Thursday there were people queuing to register, others juggling and unicycling in the main hall and the equipment sellers had their stands up.

A big round of applause came from the hall and everyone rushed to the window to see what was happening. I had to follow and saw a guy standing on top of a free standing ladder juggling so many rings I couldn't count them. I was told his name was Popovitch – from the Moscow State Circus – and that I'd missed seeing him juggle with five clubs and doing half a dozen other tricks while on the ladder. As well as this Russian representative there were lots of Americans. In fact L'Institut Francais du Jonglage seemed to consist entirely of Americans!

One of the American Raspyni Brothers juggled five knives late one evening but later when I saw them passing seven clubs I realised they may not be entirely insane. I had my doubts about François Chotard who had grown and filed his finger nails specially for ball spinning. He can spin at least eight at one time. I couldn't wait to see some of these skills used in performance but when Cirque du Trottoir (Sidewalk Circus) put on an impromptu show the crowd was so deep I couldn't see what was happening from the bar. I did hear castenets, musical instruments and wild applause and I saw the top half of a marionette sketch where the puppeteers were on stilts.

There were workshops throughout the convention on everything from devil stick and diabolo to balloon modelling. I decided to learn to juggle too. After all there were lots of girls who could do it and some were really good, like Kezia Tenenbaum of Airjazz. When I plucked up enough nerve to ask someone they were really helpful and, believe it or not, ten minutes later I could nearly juggle.

Conventions, which are held annually, help to bring juggling to a wider audience. They are also useful places to learn other circus skills such as uni-cycling (riding a one-wheeled cycle), walking on stilts and crossing a tight-rope. All these can be done while juggling given good tuition and lots of practise. Many of the juggling classes in Britain also include these skills but if you cannot find a suitable class near you there are intensive week-end or week long courses held in Bristol by *Fooltime*. This is a centre for circus skills with courses run by professional teachers and entertainers. Everything from juggling to clowning, and mime to the trapeze is taught here. For more information write to;

Fooltime
40 Thomas Street
Bristol
BS2 9LL

If you cannot get to a class, the Further reading list on page 90 provides details on books covering subjects beyond the scope of this book. We have only listed books that we know and have found useful and interesting – there are many more which have been written and your local library may be able to obtain them for you.

Probably the best place to see jugglers performing is in Covent Garden Market where, by the portico of St Paul's Church, street entertainers enthrall and amuse the crowds. There are normally a few jugglers there and most of them will be happy to talk with you about juggling and maybe even teach you some tricks. Many of the juggling acts you see in theatres or on television started out as street entertainers since it is an ideal way to develop the skills of juggling and performing needed to succeed as a professional. On the street there are the obvious advantages of plenty of space and no height restrictions although the wind and rain can cause problems.

There are a surprising number of people who know simple three-ball juggling and we have found that many people are keen to learn or improve. Gradually, as you become known as a juggler, you may find that others cannot resist the temptation to try which just goes to show that juggling is catching!

Further reading

Many of these books are published abroad but may be obtainable from the Distributers of juggling equipment found on page 89.

Juggling – The art and its artists by Karl-Heinz Zeithen and Andrew Allen.

This a costly but magnificent pictorial history of juggling for the real enthusiast, with 298 photographs and 93 illustrations. It is available from the publishers, Rausch and Lüft, Hasenheide 54, D-1000 Berlin 61, W. Germany, priced at 133Dm including postage and packing.

The Juggler's Manual of Cigar Box Manipulation & Balance and *The Juggler's Manual of Manipulative Miscellanea* by Reginald W. Bacon.

Both these books are useful as they provide comprehensive information on a range of topics seldom covered elsewhere. The first covers practically everything you can do with cigar boxes and gives clear illustrations. The second presents the classic skills with top hats, canes, plates, nesting cups and other assorted objects. Each book costs $10 including postage and packing from Variety Arts Press, PO Box 489, Newburyport, MA 01950, USA.

Circus in a Suitcase by Reg Bolton

This provides a good introduction into the skills such a uni-cycling, tight-rope walking, escapology in addition to juggling. It is a useful book for anyone working with children or doing street shows. Available from Nicky Bee.

The Buskers by David Cohen and Ben Greenwood

This is an intriguing account of the history of street entertainment from the Roman Empire to the present day. Published by David & Charles, Newton Abbot, Devon.

Circus Techniques by Hovey Burgess

As well as juggling this book covers spinning plates, trapeze, slack-rope, tight-rope, and equilibristics. Available from Brian Dubé (*see* Distributers of juggling equipment).

The Art of Juggling by Ken Benge

Covering most aspects of ball and club juggling, the highlight of this book is the instructions on over 60 different three-ball variations, with clear diagrams. Published by Anderson World Inc, Box 366, Mountain View, CA 94042, USA.

Comedy Juggling by Rich Chamberlin

Suggestions and lines for use in a comedy juggling routine. Published by The Juggling Arts, 61 Calpella Drive, San Jose, CA 95136, USA, Price $4.50 post paid.

Kascade and *Juggler's World* are both interesting and informative sources of up-to-date information. Details of obtaining these are given in Chapter 11.

Acknowledgements

There are many many people who helped us with this work. Pearse Halfpenny was particularly kind to lend us his extensive collection of juggling books and buoyed us up with his enthusiasm. Johnny and Suma Lamonte gave us an impression of what it was like to be part of a juggling family. We would also like to thank others who have helped us in various ways including Tony Green, Max and Susie, Peter Briggs, Chris Adams, Dave Spathaky, Alex Dandridge, Olly Crick, Norman Francome, Sidney Francome, Tal Jacks (Jack Taylor) and the Flying Karamazov Bros.

Index

Alternative Cabaret, 78
Anglo, 10, 11

Balancing, 55, 79, 82, 83
Beanbags, 13
Behind the back, 27, 38, 70, 76
Bounce juggling, 58, 59
Box, the, 74
Bucci, Anthony, 59

Cascade, 14-18, 24, 25, 27, 35, 57, 76
Chamberlin, Richard, 75, 76
Champagne bottles, 82
Cheats Pirouette, 70
Children's shows, 79-81
Chinese, 10, 50
Chop, 31
Chrysostomus, 10
Cigar boxes, 11, 47-9
Cinguevalli, Paul, 11
Club balance, 41
Clubs, 35-43
Columns, 14, 19-22, 39, 56
Comedy, 24
Concentration, 9
Conjurer's Monthly, 11
Comedy, 24
Crick, Ollie, 78

Devil sticks, 10, 53, 54, 87
Diabolo, 50-2, 87
Double spins, 36, 43, 68, 70
Drums, 12, 43, 81
Dummy, the, 28
Dupois, Matthieu, 10

Ear roll, 61, 77
Egg trick, 84
Egypt, 10
Elbow Catch, 28
Exercise, 9

Fields, W. C., 11
Five balls, 57
Flash, 24
Flats, 40
Flying Karamazov Bros, 12
Football (soccer), 24, 61
Foot kick up, 40, 43
Four balls, 56
Four clubs, 44

Giraffe, 34
Goldston, Will, 10
Gorilla, 33

Hamley's 11
Heading, 24, 60, 76, 77
Helicopter, 42
Holman, David, 81
Horton, T. (Anglo), 10, 11
Houdini, Harry, 11

International Juggler's Association, 87

Jugglers Bulletin, 11
Juggling, 89

Kascade, 87
Kissing, 18, 22
Knives, 10
Koch, 10

Lacrosse balls, 13, 58
Lamonte, Johnny, 75
Lamonte, Suma, 75
Long and the Short, 78

Magicians, 10, 78
Matchbox trick, 86
Mouth knockout, 70
Music hall, 10

Neck catch, 28, 76, 77

Overhead cascade, 32
Over the head, 39

Party tricks, 86
Passing, 62-74
Penguin, 33
Ping pong balls, 46
Plate spinning, 78-80

Rappo, Carl, 10
Restelli, Enrico, 11
Reverse cascade, 25, 39
Revolvers, 10
Rings, 45, 87

San Francisco, 12
Scarves, 76
Sexism, 78
Shower, 14, 23, 56, 59
Silicon balls, 13, 58
Socrates, 10
Standard start, 66

Stanyon, Prof Ellis, 10
Stealing, 63, 64

Tennis balls, 13, 58
Thorpe Park, 78
Three ball flash, 24, 57
Three ball start, 13
Three club start, 43
Three three ten, 66
Tie juggling, 85
Torches, 10, 43
Train Roll, 32
Triangle, 72-3
Triple spins, 36, 43, 44, 68-70

Under the leg, 24, 38, 69, 70
Unicycle, 87
United States, 9
Ursus, Tagatus, 10

Van Aro, Eric, 10

Yo yo, 29, 30, 50

Idealistic 'green' stance

SANE NEW WORLD: Replacing Values

By Colin Francome, published by

Carla Publications.

Price: £4.95 (paperback)

By David M. Smith

Colin Francome possesses many talents. He is an academic with an international reputation for his work on abortion. He is also renowned as a talented juggler, and London Marathon runner.

In this book he breaks new ground, combining his undoubted academic skills with his ability to communicate and entertain, in order to produce a serious and committed piece of writing aimed at a popular audience.

The book takes an idealistic 'green' stance - but green in the German sense of seeking an alternative society rather than the weaker English sense of environment concern. Rejecting what he sees as the arguments of the political right and left, he calls for 'radical changes throughout the whole of social life....moving beyond the old goals of wealth and property...to move towards a different kind of lifestyle where people's lives are far more interesting, where they can develop their talents...where crime is diminished, where health care is available for all and is carried out for the benefit of people and not the pursuit of profit.'

As an educator himself he is not particularly concerned to develop the theme of 'double alienation'. People in rich countries are educated to develop wealth rather than their own potential for creativity, and at the same time are alienated from the realities of life for people in the poorer countries.

In chapter one he sets out his argument in terms of a number of issues - wealth versus the quality of life; quality rather than quantity as the focus of production; health, environment and medicine; crime and violence; world poverty. Each of these is then addressed in more detail in a subsequent chapter.

The final chapter, entitled 'What can I do?', details action at the local, national and international level, which he believes will replace the values of the present world with a new perspective to produce a *sane new world.*

The attraction of this book is that it is serious, full of information and examples, yet is aimed at a popular audience. It would make an excellent basis for anyone concerned with running discussion groups about contemporary problems or current affairs.

It will, I believe, particularly appeal to a teenage audience in that it is relevant, different, easily comprehensible and offers them lots of the precise detail on contemporary political concerns which can really get adults' backs up.

David M. Smith is with the School of Sociology and Social Policy.